With Botha and Smuts in Africa

GENERAL BOTHA

With Botha and Smuts in Africa

No 1 Squadron of the Royal Naval Armoured
Car Division During the First World War

W. Whittall

LEONAUR

With Botha and Smuts in Africa
No 1 Squadron of the Royal Naval Armoured Car Division
During the First World War
by W. Whittall

First published under the title
With Botha and Smuts in Africa

Leonaur is an imprint of Oakpast Ltd

ISBN: 978-0-85706-964-1 (hardcover)
ISBN: 978-0-85706-965-8 (softcover)

http://www.leonaur.com

Publisher's Notes

Contents

Preface

Though this volume deals with certain aspects of two most interesting campaigns, it has not been my object to write a detailed history of either. I have rather tried to confine myself to those events on both sides of the Dark Continent which came within my own purview. Necessarily, I have strayed outside the purely personal sometimes, in order to preserve the continuities and to take a more general survey of the operations of war which added two vast and extremely valuable territories to the Empire; but I scarcely think that I need apologise to the reader on that account.

I feel that I should be doing something less than justice to them did I not take this opportunity of putting on record my sense of gratitude to the officers and men of No. 1 Squadron of the Royal Naval Armoured Car Division, which I had the honour to command, for the ungrudging devotion to duty displayed by all, often in circumstances of the greatest hardship and discomfort. In the words of the Government of the Union of South Africa they "under all conditions and in all circumstances maintained the high traditions of the Royal Navy," and worthier praise than this would be impossible. It therefore only remains for me to dedicate to them this unambitious record of the work we accomplished together.

W. W.

CHAPTER 1

After the Event

One of these days, when the greatest of all wars has passed into history, and the time has come when we can regard the "side-shows" in their true perspective, it will be granted that the campaign which added the South-West African Protectorate to the British Empire was a model of what such a campaign should be. Masterly strategy, planned by a master of war, in combination with the supremest self-sacrifice on the part of the troops engaged, enlarged the empire's possessions by more than a quarter of million square miles of territory at a cost, in life, of only 140, including deaths from all causes—battle casualties and disease.

It is obvious from the figures that the actual fighting was not on the grand scale. True it is that the casualties of the whole campaign were no more in killed and wounded than are incurred in France in an isolated trench raid, but to measure the success of a campaign by the size of the butcher's bill is to view it from an altogether wrong standpoint. As a matter of fact the reverse may often be the case. It most certainly was so in South-West Africa, where the loss of life was in inverse ratio to the results achieved. Had a less able commander than General Botha been in charge of the operations, not only would the bill have been far heavier, but the campaign must have dragged its weary length over many more months than were occupied in the conquest. The character of the campaign was exactly suited to his genius, and had a soldier trained in a less elastic school than Botha been in chief command we should quite possibly have been longer over it, and on occasion the casualty list might have been sufficiently heavy to satisfy the most exacting of that type of critics which is prone to the platitude that *you cannot make omelettes without breaking eggs.*

In brief, the story of the campaign is one of battling against the most appalling conditions of country in the endeavour to compel an elusive enemy to fight who declined to accept action except on his own terms. It must not be imagined for a moment that the garrison of South-West Africa was averse from fighting. On the contrary, on the rare occasions when conditions apparently favoured them they put up a very good fight indeed. Sandfontein, Gibeon, Riet, Trekkopjes, all bear witness to the fighting capacity of the Germans when they thought things were more or less as they wanted. For whatever the faults of the German, bad soldiership is not one of the most marked of his characteristics, and it was the fact that he was hopelessly out numbered and entirely outclassed in leadership that impelled him to decline action when he had no earthly chance of doing more than inflict problematical delay on Botha's war machine.

In point of fact, the German command did quite well. Time after time the enemy was manoeuvred out of positions which it would have been extremely costly to take by direct assault, and which he had obviously made up his mind to defend. Hunted and harassed from end to end of the country, he frequently slipped out of the trap laid for him with consummate skill. He made mistakes, as when he allowed us to advance through two hundred miles of the most difficult country—country which was simply ideal for delaying the advance of superior forces—with nothing more serious than the constant threat to do something. Even then it must be said that the German command had realised that the end was inevitable. By that time his reservists, who were mostly farmers, miners and railway workers before the war, were giving open expression to their "fed-upness." The war would be decided in Europe, they said, and there was no sense in trying to keep by fighting what they would ultimately get back automatically, *plus* an indemnity.

Colonel Franke, the German commander, could in all honour have surrendered six weeks before things had come to this pass, and it is thus hardly fair to bring up in evidence the errors of the hopeless closing phase. He was, after all, a good soldier of his misguided *Kaiser*. He kept over 50,000 Union troops in the field against him for months, and that at a time when every trained man was at his highest value to the Allied cause. Until German South-West Africa was cleaned up, the South African Union could not spare a man for any of the other theatres of war. The troops detained there were wanted—and how badly will not be known yet—in East Africa. They were wanted in

Mesopotamia; they were needed everywhere, in short. Without presuming, therefore, to pass a final judgment on the enemy conduct of the campaign from the purely military viewpoint, it may be conceded that Colonel Franke did very well indeed when all the circumstances are taken into account.

Had there been no German enemy in the field, the difficulties would have been sufficient to daunt all but the most determined of commanders. Hundreds of miles of stark desert, almost waterless and without vegetation save for occasional patches of poisonous "milk-bush" scrub; poisoned and polluted water-holes and mine-strewn tracks; scorching sun by day and frost at night; flies that were like the Egyptian plague, sand that was like marching in deep snow and, where the sand was not, rock that cut the stoutest of boots to ribbons in a week; surely these things were enough of themselves to fight against, and it was these that the enemy depended upon to fight for him, to his undoing. The genius of Botha and the astonishing tenacity of his troops were more than sufficient to negative the appalling character of the conditions under which they were called upon to fight and effective, to discount the efforts of an enemy who had been preparing for many months in advance, not so much to defend his own, but actually, with the help of the disloyal element among the Boers, to possess himself of the Union territories. But that is another story.

CHAPTER 2

Walfish Bay

Early in March, 1915, I was ordered to South-West Africa in command of a squadron of the newly-constituted R.N. Armoured Car Division. The establishment of a squadron was normally twelve "light" and three "heavy" armoured cars, with an armament of three 8-pr. quick-firers and fifteen machine-guns—a fairly powerful fighting unit under conditions favourable to the use of the new arm. In view of the conditions supposed to exist—I say supposed, because there appeared to be an utter want of reliable information about the country in which we were to work—the three heavy cars and their guns were left in England, and I took out only the twelve "light" vehicles. Incidentally, I may remark that these were in the neighbourhood of four tons in weight when ready to take the field.

The voyage out was made in the pleasantest of circumstances, as the powers that be detained a 13,000-ton Australian trooper, which had brought over a part of the Australian Contingent, to drop us at Walfish Bay on the way out to Australia, whither she was bound on another trooping trip. Thus we had the ship to ourselves, and, with ten officers and about 120 other ratings, we were certainly not overcrowded. We saw nothing in the way of shipping, save a solitary French steamer bound for St. Helena, during the whole passage, and, with fine weather from beginning to end, the voyage may be called about as uneventful as ever a trooping run was. Drills, instruction and sports made the voyage pass both quickly and pleasantly, and, almost before we had well realised that we were at sea, the sixteenth day had arrived and we were at anchor in Walfish Bay.

Walfish had been made the sea base for the Northern Force destined to co-operate in the conquest of South-West Africa. Although a British possession, and the only real harbour on the whole west coast of Africa, practically nothing has ever been done to develop it. It has been for years a whaling station of some little importance. In fact, the town, such as it is, appears to be a sort of offshoot of the whaling industry.

The most prominent features of the landscape are two groups of tall, lanky iron chimneys belonging to the whaling station and the condenser plant. The last is a very necessary part of the town economy, since there is no water supply available and every drop has to be condensed from sea water. The "town" consists of a tumbledown, ramshackle sort of building, honoured by the name of Residency, which in peaceful times housed the magistrate who was charged with the administration of the place. Cheek by jowl with the Residency is a tiny church, but I was never able to discover whether it boasted an incumbent. For the rest, a few huts suffice for the housing of the nonofficial part of the population.

It has been said that if we had only been amenable to sweet reason and handed over to the Germans Walfish and the strip of coast-line to which we clung so tightly, Swakopmund would never have been built, and we should have had the reversion of a well-planned and wellconstructed town on the only harbour on the coast. That may or may not be the case, and it is not my purpose to discuss the reasons which led us to hang on to a place of which we made no use at all in peace, but which proved invaluable in war. It is fairly certain, however, that the Germans would have made Walfish the port of South-West Africa instead of Swakopmund, which is really not a port at all, exposed as it is to the full westerly sweep of the Atlantic. Incidentally, the Germans, in return for what they called our dog-in-the-manger policy, did their best to prevent trade from passing through Walfish, even going to the length of proclaiming the desert *hinterland* a game reserve, with the purpose of preventing native trade with the British possession.

The harbour of Walfish is formed by a spit, known as Pelican Spit, which runs practically north and south and affords perfect protection to the anchorage in all winds. There is plenty of water for large ships to lie within a mile of the shore, and smooth water makes it possible to land troops and stores at any time. From the sea the country appears to recede into the far distance as a rolling *vista* of sand-dunes. Barren and inhospitable as it looks on first acquaintance, its appearance flatters it. To make its acquaintance from the sea is to dislike it. To become intimate with it from close association is to learn to hate it with all one's heart and soul. But more of this *anon*.

The Germans made haste to seize Walfish at the outbreak of the war. They took prisoners the magistrate and the solitary policeman who assisted to maintain order, but the former they released shortly afterwards. It was not until nearly five months afterwards that the British made any serious effort to regain possession of the place. As a matter of fact, except for the moral effect of the enemy's being in occupation of British territory, there was no reason why we should trouble about it. An isolated point on a sea coast, such as Walfish, is only a source of weakness to its possessors while the enemy is in occupation of the country behind it. Nothing, therefore, was done until the plans for the conquest of German South-West Africa had been matured and Walfish was needed as a *point d'appui*. Then things began to happen in fairly rapid sequence.

On Christmas Day, 1914, an expeditionary force, under the command of Colonel Skinner, and consisting of two infantry brigades with the Imperial Light Horse, Grobelaar's Scouts and an artillery brigade, landed without opposition, and made good the defences of the place against attack from Swakopmund. It seems doubtful if the landing was known to the enemy. The morning, as are most mornings on that part of the coast, was foggy, and it was not until next day, when a weak German patrol came into collision with an outpost of the Rand Rifles, that the enemy appears to have known that anything had happened. Later information leads one to the conclusion that the German Intelligence was hopelessly at fault, and that they did not expect a serious landing for at least another three weeks.

What the expeditionary force had succeeded in regaining was an excellent harbour, which proved absolutely invaluable to the objects of the campaign. But a harbour without facilities for landing is of very little account. And facilities were completely non-existent. There was a crazy jetty, with an even crazier crane, which in its youth had been capable of lifting three tons. Roads there were none. Indeed, had roads been made they would have been swallowed in the everlasting sand in a month. The German railway system ended at Swakopmund—and that place is twenty miles away. Therefore, everything had to be created, and if the South African departmental troops had accomplished nothing else in the war, the story of their work in those early days at Walfish would be monument enough of their untiring efficiency and devotion to the business in hand.

Lighters and floats to convey railway material and rolling stock ashore from the transports had to be built on the spot. A slipway for landing locomotives and other heavy gear was constructed. Water tanks had to be erected, the bulk of the water required for the troops being brought by sea from Cape Town and stored at Walfish. This alone will convey some sort of idea ct the nature of the country to which the Union troops were now committed. To be compelled to transport water 800 miles by sea is surely unique in all the annals of war!

By the time our transport arrived at Walfish quite a busy atmosphere pervaded the place. The South African Engineer Corps—who, by reason of their ability to take on any sort of job, and the wonderful rapidity with which they pushed on with railway construction, were irreverently dubbed the "Galloping Gasfitters"—had constructed a metre-gauge line to Swakopmund. True, the rails were dumped down on the sand with little or no pretence of ballasting, and the line itself looked, as someone said, more like delirious snakes than a railway, but it served its purpose well and truly. The whole of the supplies for the Northern operations were carried over this hastily-laid road right up to the end of the campaign.

Huge structures for the housing of stores had sprung into existence. Enormous quantities of forage and stores had been accumulated, and the whole life of the place was that of a great military base at which efficiency and yet more efficiency was the single end in view. It may be that the Colonial soldier goes about his job in a way that is very often, to say the least, not quite professional in its method, but after Walfish let no one tell me that he has anything to learn about practical war and its makeshifts.

The landing arrangements at Walfish were in charge of Commander Price, R.N.V.R., who was senior naval transport officer on the spot. As soon as I had been to Swakopmund and received orders to disembark, the next business was to see him and arrange about landing the cars and stores. My instructions from home were that every dispatch was to be used to release the transport, which was urgently required in Australia. Everyone was willing, but the landing staff could do nothing for us. Other ships were waiting discharge, and urgent orders were in hand that railway material and rolling stock were to have priority. There were no lumpers to be had to sling the cars out of the hold, and all the "boys" ashore were working sixteen hours a day in landing railway material. But the navy has a way of helping itself when needs be, and it was no part of our intention to be delayed, particularly as we knew that the beginning of the great advance was timed for a week later.

I found that Price could manage to spare us four pontoons, and could have them towed alongside a half-finished jetty a mile above the town if we could do the rest. So the day after we arrived we got the first pontoon alongside the ship, and began on two days as strenuous work as any of us had ever tackled. Neither officers nor men spared themselves. Twenty-two cars, to say nothing of the motorcycles and a couple of hundred tons of stores, had to be slung overside, lashed on the pontoons, and then landed on a rickety jetty whose sole accessories to landing were a few loose planks.

To add to the difficulties, there was a heavy tidal range alongside the jetty, so that the pontoons constantly surged six or more feet in both directions. This made it an exciting business to get armoured cars ashore, as the only method was to drive them under their own power across a couple of narrow planks, watching for the smooth to rush them over. However, thanks to the skill of the drivers and to a fair amount of luck, we got everything ashore without so much as wetting a package of stores, much to the astonishment of the landing staff, who expected us to take a week over the job and to land some of the cars at the bottom of the bay.

During the few days we were at Walfish we had our first experience of the fly plague. I thought I knew something about flies, but never have I seen anything to approach the Walfish brand. Inside the tents it is no exaggeration to say that you could not put a finger on the canvas without touching a fly. And for sheer pertinacity in annoyance I have never met their equals. We tried every remedy known but without avail—there was nothing to be done but to endure the plague with as much resignation as one could put into it.

In the meantime orders came through that I was to proceed to Swakopmund, where General Botha had his headquarters, to discuss the disposition of the squadron in the coming advance, so I left Nalder, my second in command, in charge and went on to Swakop by motor-trolley over the new railway. Why the vehicle kept on the rails for a hundred yards has always been a bit of a mystery to me, but it did, and we bumped and banged over the twenty miles in very little more than an hour.

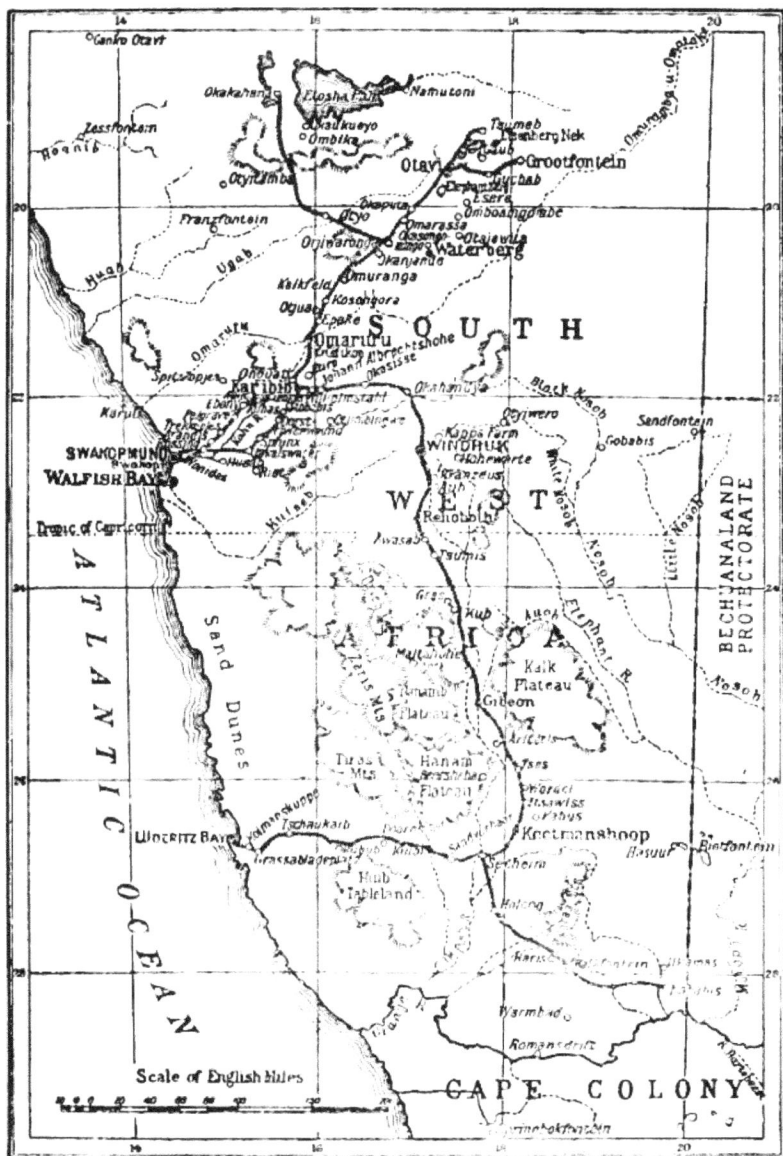

SKETCH MAP OF SOUTH-WEST AFRICA

Chapter 3

Swakopmund and the General

Approached either from Walfish by the railway or from the sea, Swakopmund reminds one irresistibly of the White City. It is at once wonderful and grotesque—wonderful in its demonstration of German thoroughness, grotesque in its evidence that that thoroughness is of the sealed-pattern variety which says: "Here we will build a town. Never mind about anything else; we will see to it that it be like other German towns."

Swakopmund is a town of imposing buildings, quite out of keeping with the country in which it has been dumped down. In normal times it had a population of about 1,800 whites and a post office that would have served a third-rate European city. The hospital—another example of the sealed pattern—is large enough to have served the whole white population of the Colony. Everything appears to have been done on the same lavish scale, so that one ceases to wonder that the German African colonies had always been a heavy financial liability instead of a paying proposition.

The town was occupied, practically without opposition, by Colonel Skinner's column on January 14th, 1915. It had been fairly well cleared of all valuable and portable property by the Germans themselves before their evacuation of the place, so that the stories which became current of the looting that was allowed after the British occupation are quite devoid of truth. All enemy property was taken over by a public works department which was immediately constituted. Whatever was required for the use of the troops was commandeered and issued on proper requisition by responsible officers. Such buildings as were needed for administrative purposes or for the accommodation of the troops were taken into use, and before many days were past Swakopmund had settled down into as orderly a military community as though the Union troops had been in occupation of the place for years. Their discipline was eloquent of their soldierliness.

When I reached Swakopmund, G.H.Q. was established in the former premises of the Woermann Line, which included quite palatial residential quarters as well as the necessary business accommodation. The Colonial Hun certainly knows how to do himself well, whatever may be his other shortcomings. General Botha did not occupy the Woermann building, a residence close at hand, belonging to one of the chiefs of the firm, having been impressed for his use and that of the personal staff.

Immediately on arrival I reported to Colonel Collyer, the chief Staff officer. Collyer is an old Cape Mounted Rifleman and, as is the case with all C.M.R. officers, rose from the ranks, and reached his present responsible position—he is now chief of staff to General Smuts in East Africa—by sheer force of ability. We discussed the possibility of the cars accompanying the main advance up the Swakop River. Before we left England I had said I believed it was possible to take armoured cars anywhere that guns could go, but a very few days in this appalling country of sand and desolation had made me a great deal less of an optimist in that regard.

As a matter of fact, had it been possible to traverse in advance the country over which we ultimately worked, I should have said that it was a waste of time and effort to try it. However, that is by the way. Collyer opined that we could not hope to negotiate the bed of the river, which does duty for road for the first fifty miles ot Swakopmund. I was perfectly willing to try, and said that, as the column was going to use motor transport, I was sure we could do it. The discussion ended with the advice that I should go up the railway as far as Nonidas, about eleven miles from Swakopmund, and prospect the country.

Next day I secured a motor-trolley from the railway staff and went out to Nonidas. There I found two subalterns of the Motor Transport, who scoffed at the idea of our being able to use the cars at all. It took them all their time, they said, to get through the sand with stripped touring chassis, and as earnest of this I was taken about ten miles out on the "road" which such motor transport as was then in use had to take. What I saw was not the least bit encouraging. The sand was bottomless, and, worst of all, it was a sand in which the wheels could get no bite.

The surface formation of the country is a rotten red granite, desiccated by the dry climate of ages, and contains a large proportion of mica. The sand, therefore, is as fluid almost as water, and will not "pack" under the wheels. Once the car comes to a standstill it is hopeless to ask it to get away again without strenuous manhandling. Later we learnt how to get over the trouble, but in the first stages of our noviotiate we sometimes had appalling difficulty in negotiating the drifts and river beds.

The river beds are a peculiar feature of the country. At some time or other there must have been a good deal of water, even in the Namib desert, for the beds of streams and rivers occur at least every half-mile or so, but no rain has fallen in the coast belt to account for even the smallest of these within living memory. It is on record that a little rain fell about ten years ago!

I returned to Swakopmund late in the afternoon, not at all hopeful of the prospect, and found that in the meantime matters had been settled for us. I was to detach my wireless telegraphy car and some details to accompany headquarters, and, with the whole of the armoured cars, to join up with Colonel Skinner's column, the 3rd Infantry Brigade, which was then at Trekkopjes, about forty miles up the Otavi Railway. The idea was that the cars were to be railed up to Nonidas, and were then to proceed by "road." By representing that it would save a great deal of time, I managed to get sanction to take them by train to railhead, which was then just short of Trekkopjes, and being pushed ahead at the rate of some ten kilometres a day. Nalder remained in charge of entraining the cars and stores at Walfish, while I stayed on at Swakopmund, collecting all the information possible regarding the country and worrying the railway staff for trucks.

One of the most remarkable things about my quest for information was that no one seemed to know a thing about the interior. As I have recorded, I had been no farther in than Nonidas on the one road and to "Kilo. 40" on the other. Certainly up to there the prospects were bad enough to cause the most serious misgiving, but everywhere I was assured that the farther one went in from the coast the better the conditions became. At Nonidas I had met a cheery captain of the Kimberley Regiment who had not been up there himself, but who averred that beyond Rossing the country was splendid for cars. Good hard going, and surface like an English main road! At Rossing it was the same. "Of course, it's pretty rotten going here, but wait till you get to Arandis. It's magnificent going from there, and you'll be able to take your cars anywhere."

In the result, we *were* able to take the cars anywhere, but no thanks to Nature, which seemed to have designed the country with an eye to keeping motorcars from traversing it. During the whole campaign we did not encounter five miles of road that by any stretch of the imagination could be called even passably fit for cars. Certainly we never discovered the perfect motoring country that always lay ten or fifteen miles ahead of us.

During my stay at Swakopmund I met General Botha for the first time. The meeting was the more interesting in that it was not at all of an official character, but simply a social interlude in the serious business of preparing for the advance. The invitation to meet him came through a message from one of the personal staff to the effect that the general would be pleased if I would go to tea with him that afternoon.

I had heard a great deal about Botha and his wonderful influence among his own people. It was well understood that a very large proportion of the burgher troops were not at all keen on being commandeered to serve outside the Union, and, in fact, many whose opinions were worth having anticipated that, unless the campaign were short and decisive, there might be trouble on account of the very natural desire of the Boers to get back to their farms, which were falling into decay while they were away fighting in a quarrel which very many regarded as none of their business. It must be remembered in this connection that it was only twelve years since these same people were at war against us, and that even now the memory rankles in some quarters.

Then, too, there had been the recent rebellion to revive controversy, so that, to say the least, it was a daring thing to have risked putting the commandeering law into effect for the purposes of the war in South-West Africa. Nothing but the tremendous influence and personality of Louis Botha could have justified it. The whole of the burgher articles of faith, so far as this aspect of the matter is concerned, was summed up in the very simple formula: "Louis Botha says so."

This is not in the least an exaggerated view, but the soberest of truth, as I was subsequently able to ascertain by many discussions with Dutch and British members of the Union forces, I knew also that Louis Botha was held in real affection by the members of his staff, both personal and general, but it was not until I met him that I was able to understand the reason of his extraordinary power over men. And even then, though I could understand and appreciate it to the full, I could not pretend to define exactly what it is that produces or

21

General Smuts

accounts for his influence.

Simple and unaffected as he is in manner, no one can meet and talk to Botha for five minutes without coming under the spell of his magnetic personality. He compels you at once to the conviction that this is indeed a leader of men. Charming and direct in conversation, he impresses you as one who is absolutely sure of himself, and inspires you with equal confidence in him. There is an undefinable and subtle something about him—some elusive quality which cannot be put into words, but which makes you cease to wonder what it is that has made him the trusted and revered leader of his people. And, even so, you do not know why.

It is this quality of the man which, for want of a better term, one must can personal magnetism—though it falls far short of being descriptive of it—that kept the Boers in the field against us during the South African War, when, under a less compelling leader, they would have abandoned a hopeless fight a year before they did. It was this same quality of leadership at its best that sustained Botha's burghers and the astonishing South African infantry in the desert marches of the South-West African campaign.

CHAPTER 4

Into the Desert

A week after our first arrival at Walfish we were well on our way to Trekkopjes. Not bad going either, considering that we had to entrain all the cars and stores without assistance from an improvised ramp, and that rolling stock was necessarily at a premium. It is no easy matter to stow two 4-ton cars in a metre-gauge open truck with no lifting gear to assist. But everybody put his back into it—we hadn't come all the way from England to lose any of the campaign by sitting down to look at work—and once again I think we rather surprised the staff at Walfish by the celerity with which things were done.

Before I left Swakopmund I had to undergo a lot of good-natured ragging from the staff. It was never anticipated that the Germans would have the temerity to come down and attack Colonel Skinner on the railway. As a matter of fact, so little was it anticipated that on the very day I left for Trekkopjes two naval 12-pounders, which were the only guns Skinner had with him, were withdrawn to take part in the main advance through Riet. The staff was on this account very sympathetic, and professed much sorrow that we were to be marooned in a quarter of the theatre in which there was going to be no show at all. They tried to console us for the prospect by promising to drive the garrison of Karibib down to us, so that we should at least get a run for our money. A party of them saw us off, and as a parting shot one said: "Well, so long, boys! Listen for the sound of our guns about Thursday and wish you were with us!"

What they did not foresee was that on the Tuesday *they* would be anxiously listening at the telephone to the sound of the enemy's guns attacking *us* in the one really serious action that was to take place before German South-West Africa became a British protectorate. But so it befell, as will appear later.

Swakopmund itself is built among the dunes, and only by constant labour is it able to keep its head above the sand. It has its own brand of climate, which can best be described in the one word poisonous. The sea is ice-cold all the year round—as those who tried bathing discovered. There is no rain to speak of, but more than sufficient humidity is provided through the medium of the sea fogs which are of almost daily occurrence. Thus there is an alternation of bitterly cold and piercing mist—which seems to search one's very marrow—and scorching sunshine. Usually the morning is cold and foggy, but towards noon the sun has gathered strength enough to clear away the fog, and the afternoon is hot enough to satisfy a salamander. Ten miles or so from the coast the influence of the cold Atlantic is lost, and the fogs do not occur at all.

For the first sixty miles the whole terrain is a howling desert of red granite and volcanic rock, with here and there patches of milk-bush scrub. The milk-bush—I never heard its real name—is a plant that grows in long, fleshy spines about three to four feet high. The spines exude when broken an ill-smelling, milky fluid which causes intense irritation when applied to the skin. How it manages to grow at all, let alone to contain the moisture it does, passes understanding. Anyway, it affords relief to the eye from the eternal vista of sun-scorched rock and sand, broken at intervals by *kopjes* that only serve to accentuate the utter aridness of the country.

There is not a drop of water in the sixty miles. The map shows a few alleged water-holes, but in none of them was there water, and the whole of the water for men and animals of the northern column had to be railed up from Nonidas, at which there had been established a water station which drew its supplies from the bed of the Swakop River. And such water it was! Brackish was no name for it, and even boiled and made into tea it was unpalatable to the last degree, and caused a good deal of stomach trouble among the troops who were compelled to drink it. Supplies, too, were very limited, the allowance per man being half a gallon a day for all purposes—when it was available, which was not always.

Water was from the start the chief difficulty, and remained so throughout all the campaign. Often the objective of the day's march was a water-hole which the Intelligence maps assured us had "permanent water." Arrived there, the water had no existence, and the weary troops would push on for another ten miles to the next alleged water-hole, too often to find that this again failed them. I had had the water problem in mind from the beginning, and had secured in Swakopmund a number of steel beer-kegs left behind by the Germans. They were very light and held about eleven gallons each, so that they were just what we required and proved invaluable later. *Apropos* of these same kegs, when Swakopmund was first occupied a number of them were used in conjunction with sandbags to consolidate the defences of the town. They were full of some liquid or other, but no one took the trouble to investigate the contents for some time, till one day a man jabbed his bayonet into one and out gushed—beer. Needless to say, it was not long before the good news spread round the force, and by next day there were very few full kegs left.

Since the fight at Nonidas at the end of February the principal efforts of the Union forces had been devoted to the concentration of the necessary material for the reconstruction of the Otavi Railway. This was originally a two-foot gauge line, built primarily for bringing down the produce of the Kahn and Otavi copper mines. The enemy had destroyed this as he retreated into the interior, blowing up the bridges and culverts and tumbling the line, sleepers and all, down the embankment. At intervals he provided a surprise packet in the shape of mines laid in or beside the embankment. He had, however, shockingly bad luck with these, for they were generally either found by our patrols and dug up, or else failed to explode when they were intended. I do not think that from first to last a single fighting man was killed by mining operations on the railway. Narrow escapes there were in plenty, but nothing worse.

The narrow-gauge line was replaced by the Cape metre-gauge as fast as material and stock became available. Skinner's column moving slowly forward as the line progressed. At the time we were ordered to join him his force was practically "in the air." In the event of the enemy's deciding to concentrate and seriously attack him, his only support could have been from Swakopmund, between forty and fifty miles away, at the end of a hastily constructed railway which was badly supplied with rolling stock, and that by no means of the best. Twelve hours was good going from Swakop to Trekkopjes, and there was no certainty of that, owing to the effect of the "brack" water on the locomotive boilers. It was a quite ordinary occurrence for an engine to come to a full stop between Rossing and Arandis because of the failure of its water supply due to priming.

That meant that the whole traffic of the line was held up while an engine and water tank were sent up to its relief from Nonidas. Sometimes the relief engine would fail from one cause or another, and then something very nearly approaching chaos ensued. At railhead was an infantry brigade absolutely dependent on the working of the railway for every pound of supplies and, what was infinitely worse, every drop of water. At Swakopmund and Nonidas stores and railway material were accumulating for transport to railhead and causing congestion there, while all the work of the line was held up by the failure of a single engine. They were anxious times for everyone, but the fates were certainly with us, for always, just when the position appeared to have become practically hopeless, the opportune happened and the railway got going again. We joined up with Colonel Skinner on April 24th at Trekkopjes. From a defensive point of view the camp was about as hopeless as could be imagined. It lay in a slight hollow, with a ridge to the right and a group of *kopjes* on the left front, from which the place is named.

The ground in front was covered with rocks and scrub, making it possible for an attacking force to get within charging distance under almost perfect cover. To add to the disadvantages, the ground was so hard that it was only possible to construct the shallowest of trenches. Add to this that the only two effective guns had been withdrawn on the 23rd, and some idea can be formed of the unpreparedness of the column to resist a seriously-meant attack. It was no fault of the brigadier that things were like this. His first task was to guard the railway and see that it was pushed forward with all speed. This meant that he was not free to select the best defensive position on every occasion. He had protested against his guns being taken from him, and had told G.H.Q. that he expected to be attacked. G.H.Q. scouted the idea, as I have recorded already, and had disaster overtaken Skinner's force, as it nearly did, the blame would certainly not have lain with him.

In the event, he was attacked very heavily on the morning of April 26th. On the previous night Skinner himself proceeded with a squadron of the Imperial Light Horse to reconnoitre the road towards Ebony, at which there was known to be a strong German post with guns. The force left in camp consisted of the 2nd Transvaal Scottish, 2nd Kimberley Regiment, and three out of the four sections of my own armoured car squadron, a total of some 900 rifles. Skinner's reconnaissance followed the northern side of the railway, until near Ebony his advance guard reported a strong body of the enemy with guns, moving in the opposite direction, parallel with the railway to the south.

The meeting was an entire surprise to Skinner and his party, and the Germans apparently never knew until long afterwards what a chance someone had missed. So sudden was the encounter that some of the Imperial Light Horsemen stumbled so close to the enemy that a German officer, mistaking them in the dark for his own people, peremptorily ordered them to keep in line!

Some think that Skinner ought to have attacked then. Possibly an attack might have succeeded. There would have been this in favour of such a course, that it would obviously have taken the enemy completely by surprise. However, he decided otherwise, and the force returned hurriedly to Trekkopjes to await attack there.

The 1st Rhodesian Regiment, about 450 strong, was at Arandis, some ten miles below Trekkopjes. They were ordered up, and arrived after the attack had begun in time to occupy the high ground on the right of the camp. Guns were wired for to Swakopmund, but these, in the shape of two 4-inch and two 12-pr. naval guns, did not arrive until late in the day, after the enemy had withdrawn.

The ball opened at about 6 o'clock in the morning, when an enemy detachment blew up the line about a mile in advance of the camp. It appeared afterwards that the German explosion party had been detailed to cut the railway behind us, in order to prevent guns and reinforcements from coming up, but in the dark they mistook the landmarks, and so brought quite a sporting effort to nought. Shortly after the explosion on the line the German guns opened on the camp. There were two batteries of them, and they made exceedingly good practice, the ranging being well-nigh perfect and few of their shells failing to burst.

For a considerable time they devoted their attention quite harmlessly to shelling the few tents that had been left standing, ignoring almost altogether the trenches and the Rhodesian position on the ridge. By this time we had five of our armoured cars out at distances up to half a mile in front of the fire trenches. Two others were posted in support of the infantry at the point on the railway where the trenches occupied by the Scottish and the Kimberleys joined. The other two were in reserve with the transport, which was formed up ready to move in case of a retirement.

Towards 8 o'clock the enemy apparently felt satisfied that his guns had sufficiently prepared the way for an infantry attack, and this was accordingly launched. His obvious intent was to cross the line and occupy the ridge held by the Rhodesians, which would have enabled him to enfilade the whole of our line of trenches. His advance towards the line, however, brought him under the fire of the machine-guns of the five cars which were out in front. The direction of attack was bent more towards our front by this fire, which caused a good many casualties in the German ranks.

The enemy was not to be denied, however, and again essayed to cross the line a few hundred yards lower down. Once more the fire from the cars deflected him from his line, and he bent outwards again, to make a third and then a fourth attempt to cross nearer to the camp. Both attempts were checked and defeated by the cars. The effect of the fourth and last repulse from the railway itself was to bring the enemy well across the line of our trenches and thus expose him to the full front of fire of the infantry, who then got the chance for which they had been waiting all the morning. The cover, however, was so good that it is doubtful whether the Germans suffered much from the infantry fire at this stage of the action.

Apparently not liking the cars, which were a complete surprise— they had been reported by an aeroplane observer who had been over the camp two days before as "water-carts"—the enemy abandoned his attempt to cross the railway and decided on a frontal attack on the trenches. This was launched towards 10 o'clock, after a heavy artillery preparation, which did very little harm. One battery concentrated on the cars, but although they were hit repeatedly by shrapnel only one was damaged at all seriously. Even this was put right on the next day, so the amount of damage we sustained was by no means commensurate with the enemy's expenditure of ammunition and effort.

The infantry attack was pushed with considerable resolution, many of the Germans getting to within fifty yards of the trenches, but the fire of our own infantry and that of the two supporting cars was more than they could face, and by 10.30 a.m. it was clear that the attack had failed. A counter-attack was ordered, but could make little headway without artillery support in face of the German guns, which came into action to cover the retirement. At 11.30 it was all over, and the enemy withdrew in very leisurely fashion towards Karub.

It had been a very severe action while it lasted, and at one time it looked very much as though the enemy's attack must succeed. Thanks to the steadiness of the untried South African regiments, who bore without the slightest wavering a heavy artillery fire to which we had no means of reply, and to the unexpected presence of the armoured cars with their heavy volume of machine-gun fire, it did not succeed; but it was a near thing. The enemy outnumbered us, according to one estimate, by 50 *per cent.*, and had the support of two very well served batteries; so, taking into consideration the position we had to defend, and the means at our disposal, we had reason to congratulate ourselves on the result.

The Germans left a few prisoners in our hands, and from these we gathered that they had not given up the hope of driving us back into the sea. They still appeared to hold an abiding faith in their navy, and were fully confident—in spite of the fact that they knew all about the Falkland Islands[1] battle—that before long relief would come from Europe. They were a very well set-up lot, too, with brand new equipment and clothing, and seemed to want for nothing. Their water-bottles contained a mixture of half rum, half water, from the effects of which more than one was patently suffering. None of them appeared to be particularly sorry to have fallen into our hands; in fact, one officer openly expressed his satisfaction at the fortune that had removed him from the dangers and discomforts of campaigning.

Generally speaking, they were a pretty ill-favoured lot as to physiognomy, and as sullen in demeanour as they looked. Of course, none of them had the least doubt about the final issue of the war, but there was no quarrel about that, for, equally, we had none. It was from one of these prisoners that I first heard the story, current throughout the colony, of the capture of London by the Germans! It was no use to try to get the idea out of his head. To all the reasons one could advance as to why the story should be untrue, his reply was: "You believe your news, don't you? Then why shouldn't we believe ours?" Quite unanswerable, too.

---

1. *The Battle of the Falkland Islands 1914:* the Royal Navy at war in the South Atlantic in the early days of the First World War by H. Spencer-Cooper is also published by Leonaur.

CHAPTER 5

Mines

In one respect South-West Africa must have set up a record. This was in the promiscuous use of mines by the enemy. Mines are a perfectly legitimate engine of war when they are used to effect a military purpose, but it is beyond question that the Germans overstepped the usages of civilised war in this as in so many other directions.

The country was a veritable storehouse of explosives. How many tons of dynamite and blasting gelatine we captured and dug out of the earth, where it had been planted for the purpose of blowing us off it, I should not care even to hazard an estimate of, but it was a very substantial quantity, as will appear. The possession of all this high explosive was not a part of the German preparation for war. It was merely a piece of fortuitous luck for them, though in the event it availed them very little.

The country being almost entirely devoid of any surface water supply, of necessity water could only be obtained from wells and boreholes. In consequence of the hard, rocky formations blasting was almost invariably necessary in sinking for water, and thus every farmstead and dwelling had its own stock of explosives, generally dynamite. That the enemy would fail to make use of such a material help as a practically inexhaustible stock of high explosives was not to be expected. Make use of it he did, for he literally sowed the whole country with mines, and that the Union forces did not suffer very severely as a consequence was due to a consistent good luck that scarcely fell short of a special dispensation of Providence in their favour.

Hairbreadth escapes amounting almost to the miraculous were so ordinary that they almost ceased after a time to excite comment, and the digging up and exploding of mines came to be regarded as being just as much in the day's work as the watering of animals. So contemptuous of them did everyone become that even where mines were known to have been laid no one worried to avoid the area, because of the abiding faith we had in our luck and of the utter disbelief that a German mine could by any possibility explode as its layers had designed it to do. On rare occasions they did achieve the unexpected, but even then our fortune held, and instead of losing forty or fifty men, as we should have done had the enemy's luck not been so badly out, I do not think that any one mine ever killed more than three men. I question whether the total casualties from mines came to more than fifty during the whole campaign.

Both observation and contact mines were freely used, but the latter type, naturally, predominated. These were of two kinds, both very simple and, one would have thought when seeing the detonating arrangements, very effective in their working. The commonest usually had a charge of about forty sticks of dynamite, designed to be fired by a home-made detonator which really ought to have done its work every time. It was made of a four-way union of inch or inch and a quarter gas tubing which contained a loose chemical substance in one arm of the cross. On this rested a very thin glass tube filled with a liquid which, theoretically at least, detonated the chemical on contact. Three arms of the cross were closed by screw caps, but the fourth was left open to receive a pointed steel pin, which rested in a bed of putty to keep it from breaking the glass tube until someone stepped on the striker. To ensure the striker being given every chance it was usually furnished with a flat circular plate, about eight inches in diameter. The mine would be buried in the chosen locality, with the striker-plate of the detonator lightly covered with earth, and then, if everything went according to programme, the first man or animal to step on the plate would set off the mine.

The other variety of contact mine was one that we called the "box-mine." This really consisted of two boxes, one containing the charge and the exploding detonator, the last being connected by a two-seconds length of Bickford fuse to a detonator in the other box. The latter was always buried in such a situation that our people would reach it before the one containing the charge. Its lid was supported on four light pegs, so that when it was stepped upon it collapsed, fired the detonator which lit the fuse, and if all went well the mine went up just when you had had time to reach the second box. It was a clever device, but it had the weakness that it seldom worked quite as the cheerful Hun intended.

The observation mines were usually fired in the ordinary way, by means of a battery and key, but in one or two instances a cruder form, fired by pistol and trigger wire, was used, but again neither of these had any success to speak of.

At the occupation of Swakopmund three observation mines were exploded under what ought to have been the most favourable conditions for causing serious loss to the British. The observer, who was undoubtedly a plucky fellow, had made himself a very snug hiding-place out of a harmless-looking packing-case, in which he had installed his firing gear. He succeeded in getting off his three mines. Two of them did no damage at all; the third killed two men.

A week or so afterwards a patrol which had halted to rest had dismounted, and one of the troopers thought he heard a metallic sound from underfoot, and on investigating found that he had actually been standing on the striker of a mine. Needless to say, he didn't remain long.

One of the most miraculous of all the mine escapes was that of a whole squadron of one of the mounted brigades, near Jakalswater, who had off-saddled in a clearing. They had been there for some time when one of their number noticed a man in the bush who appeared to be tugging at a line. Not dreaming of what he was doing, a few of the *burghers* thought it was, nevertheless, just as well to see into it and quietly surrounded the man, who turned out to be a German. What he was tugging at was the trigger-wire of a mine containing enough dynamite to efface the whole squadron, but, providentially, the wire had fouled a stump!

Again, at Tschaukaib, the water tanks supplying the railway had been packed with dynamite before the Germans retired, and our people had been working on them for a considerable time before the fact was discovered. At Kalkfontein a surprise had been prepared for our troops in the shape of bombs placed in the houses, designed to be exploded by cords affixed to the doors. The cords were noticed before any of the houses were entered, and ingress by the windows was the order of the day. No wonder the Germans said that the luck was all against them!

The extent to which the country was mine-sown may be judged by the fact that Colonel Skinner's force at one period of the operations dug out no fewer than eighty mines between Trekkopjes and Ebony, a distance of twenty miles, while later fifty-three were discovered in the railway embankment north of Ebony, all in a four-mile stretch. The discovery of the last batch was an example of the Providence that watched over the Union troops. An officer was captured by our mounted troops near Otjimbingwe, and among the papers in his possession was a report indicating the exact position of each of the fifty-three mines. The report was sent on to Colonel Skinner, but neither he nor any of those with him believed it to be authentic, or that, plentiful as dynamite seemed to be, the Germans would use it as prolifically as the report indicated was the case. At the same time, it would have been the sheerest folly not to have investigated things, and well it was that it was done, since the report turned out to be correct to the last detail.

Another providential escape was that of Colonel Brennan, commanding the South African Irish, at Sphinx Siding. He was driven in a motorcar over a series of mines in which 450 sticks of dynamite had been used, with ten contact points placed across eight feet of road. The wheels of the car brushed and exposed two of the contacts without exploding anything, and thus led to the timely discovery of the trap prepared for our advancing troops.

In the final operations leading up to the German surrender, we discovered in Eisenberg Nek a line of mines, laid like a snake trail, along 150 yards of road and blew them up harmlessly, except for the accidental wounding of a staff officer who was some hundreds of yards away. By all the probabilities we ought to have lost quite a number of men but for the fortunate discovery of the mine-field, for that is what it was. Instances such as I have given of the futility of the enemy's mining activities could be multiplied almost indefinitely, but I will only quote one more, which is to some extent personal and indicative of the luck that attended us in this particular.

When 9 in consequence of the progress of railway construction, it became necessary to move the brigade forward from Trekkopjes, Colonel Skinner decided on Karub as the next camping-place. At his request I accompanied him in a reconnaissance of the new camp site, and after our inspection of the ground we walked up and down in front of the railway station for a full quarter of an hour, discussing various matters. Nothing happened, and mines were about the thing farthest from our thoughts. Next day I sent an officer, with two armoured cars, to support the railhead protection party, and his report in the evening was of more than a little interest to the brigadier and myself.

It appeared that while this officer was standing in the doorway of a station a passing *Kafir* stepped full on the striker of a mine and set off the detonator. Fortunately, the main charge failed to explode. Thirty-five sticks of dynamite and two slabs of gelatine were dug out of this mine, and when we came to examine the place it was clear that on the previous day Colonel Skinner and I must have walked straight over the mine at least twenty times.

At first measures were taken for sweeping suspected areas with mule-drawn harrows, the mules being harnessed so that they hauled from the sides of the road and well clear of the possible mines. Later, in view of the rapidity of the advance, and, to some extent, I suppose, because of the contempt with which we came to regard the menace, even this precaution was ruled out, and we just took our chances. And I think we may fairly claim that the luck of the game was with us all the way along.

CHAPTER 6

Up the Swakop Valley

In order to preserve a proper perspective of the preliminary operations which made possible the final victorious advance, it is necessary now to follow the fortunes of the right and centre columns of what was called the Northern Force, of which Colonel Skinner's 3rd Infantry Brigade formed the left, or northernmost, column.

It may be remarked that really very little was known about the interior of the country that we were to invade. The German system of heavily taxing the non-German trader had not encouraged even the most enterprising of the South African business community to develop commercial intercourse. South-West Africa, whatever its possibilities in other directions, is certainly not an attractive country to the big game hunter. The larger antelopes abound, particularly in the north of the protectorate, and it is on record that a very few lions are to be seen near the Portuguese border. But of the real African big game, it may be said that it is conspicuous mainly by its absence. Therefore, the country had been avoided by that best of all intelligence workers, the hunter-explorer.

There did exist an official intelligence work, but the information was for the most part hopelessly inaccurate, particularly in the matter of water supplies, which was really the most important factor of all. It came to be a standing belief that when the intelligence book said there was permanent water at any particular place—except at the larger towns—it was quite safe to conclude that either there was no water at all or, at best, water of a very temporary character. Admittedly, it is exceedingly difficult to collect accurate data in a country which is two-thirds howling desert and is, moreover, in possession of a military power whose intentions are well-known to its own officers, with the result that the latter are at all times on the alert to prevent anything in the shape of accurate intelligence work from being done by the potential enemy. All the same, I do think that those who were responsible for the information contained in the official work had been subjected to more than the average amount of leg pulling.

Fortunately, the country had been mapped with German thoroughness, and, the maps being available to the Union Intelligence Department, the shortcomings of the guide-book were to a very great extent discounted. But even the best of maps cannot compensate for want of accurate information about the character of the country in which troops have to operate. In a previous chapter I have touched upon this want of knowledge in so far as it affected my own unit. It was the same all through. No one knew what was in front. As a matter of fact, it is not altogether certain that this was all to the disadvantage of the operations. The Germans, who did know all about the country, did not believe until the invasion was an accomplished fact that Botha would dare to move in from the coast. There was, in the days before the British occupation of the place, a German newspaper published in Swakopmund, and the Hun view of the probabilities was well expressed in its columns shortly before the arrival of the British. What it said on the subject was this:

"We do not think the British will establish themselves permanently in Swakopmund. There is nothing to be got here, and to make Swakopmund a base for invading the interior seems, to those who know the country, to be without the least prospect of success. The British will probably content themselves with hoisting the Union Jack and steaming away."

The more one regards the character of the country which had to be traversed by the invading columns the more is one inclined to agree with the German editor that, to those who know it, invasion seems to hold out no prospect of success. But then, we didn't know the country. Possibly that made just the necessary difference. I do know this, that my own officers and myself were fully agreed, when discussing things after the event, that had it been possible for us to reconnoitre in advance the country and the "roads" over which we subsequently worked, we should never have landed the cars at Walfish. We should most certainly have pronounced the country utterly impossible for any kind of motor traction, let alone for armoured cars.

But day by day we learnt more about the best methods of countering the difficulties, and day by day we consoled ourselves with the thought that the conditions simply *must* improve before long. And so it went on to the end, when everyone was surprised at what had actually been accomplished. One prepared for the very worst, and, therefore, when something that fell short of being really the worst was met with, this something was surmounted with comparative ease. I really believe that this sort of feeling, which was mostly born of sheer ignorance of the conditions in front, contributed not a little to the success of the campaign.

It has already been recorded that when the advance began the left column under Skinner was already forty miles from Swakopmund, at Trekkopjes, where we will leave it for the time being. It will come into the picture again, but it is now necessary to review the wide series of operations that led to the fall of Karibib, the enemy's principal railway centre, and Windhuk, the capital of the colony.

The Battle of Riet had been fought and won on March 20th, resulting in the capture of strong strategical positions on the main line of advance to the two places named. Had sufficient transport been available then, General Botha would have been in a position to push forward at once. The affair that culminated in the capture of Riet and Jakalswater had been initiated more as a feeler of the real strength of the German opposition than as a serious attempt to turn them out of a position it was believed they would defend to the uttermost. The first intention was to have made the main advance up the Otavi railway, in which case the Riet position would have to be taken, since it would have been fatal to leave a strong enemy force within easy striking distance of the right flank of the advance, but it was never anticipated that the German resistance would crumple up as it did. However, the necessary transport to carry out the advance as decided upon after Riet was not available, and the main force had to be withdrawn to Swakopmund while it was collected, in consequence of the absence of water at Riet itself.

In the meantime, the engineers were kept busy in the erection of tanks and motor-pumps at Riet and Husab, by which a more or less precarious supply was maintained from boreholes sunk in the bed of the Swakop River. It should be explained that the "rivers" of the country are rivers by courtesy only. Until one gets well up into the northern part of the colony the rivers are nothing but sandy beds, with no vestige of water at any time of the year. In the case of a few of the larger ones it is sometimes possible to obtain a very limited amount by sinking boreholes in the sand. Occasionally, but not often, a little can be got by digging down for ten feet or so.

While transport and supplies were being collected, Riet was occupied by Colonel Wylie's 4th Infantry Brigade, composed of the 1st Durban Light Infantry, the Rand Rifles, and the South African Irish. The duties that fell to this brigade were onerous in the extreme. In front of them was an enemy whose enterprise had by no means been knocked out of him by his severe initial reverse, and who kept the brigade constantly on the alert by threatened attacks at every part of the line. Food was scarce in the early days of the occupation, while water was almost literally worth a guinea a drop. Conditions soon began to improve, however, as it had been decided to make Riet the advanced supply depot preparatory to the great advance, and at length a vast accumulation of stores was concentrated there.

Why the enemy, who was in considerable force at the time, did not seriously attack is one of the mysteries of the campaign. Had he shown more enterprise there is no doubt at all that he could have much delayed the advance. As it was, there was only one affair worth mentioning. He did on one occasion summon up enough initiative to attack the post at Jakalswater and scored a slight momentary success, but it availed him nothing more than the capture of a couple of prisoners, who were almost instantly retaken by our people.

The force which was to move on Karibib was made up of the 1st and 2nd Mounted Brigades under Brigadier-General Brits, with Colonels Lemmer and Alberts commanding brigades; the 3rd Mounted Brigade under Brigadier-General Myburgh; the 5th Mounted Brigade under Brigadier-General Manie Botha; Wylie's infantry brigade; and detachments of artillery under Major Taylor, of the Transvaal Artillery.

Leaving Nonidas on the day after Skinner's fight at Trekkopjes, Brits moved rapidly through Riet on Dorstriviermund, following the bed of the Swakop. In the meantime Myburgh and Manie Botha had been sent off *"into the blue,"* the mission assigned to them being to cut the railway between Karibib and Windhuk at Wilhelmstahl, some thirty miles west of Karibib. Near Dorstriviermund the enemy carried out one of his few successful mine operations of the campaign, a party of Germans exploding an observation mine which killed three scouts of the Middelburg Commando. Out of this occurrence arose one of those humorous incidents which illustrate so vividly that even the grim business of war has its tighter side.

During the night after the explosion two of the advanced files were riding together, with loose knees and slack reins, the men very probably discussing the fate of their comrades, when suddenly in the moonlight a huge baboon jumped into view on a rock in front of them and gave two loud, guttural barks. Probably it did sound like the *burgher* challenge: "*Wies da?*"

At any rate, one of the men obviously thought the enemy had sprung a complete surprise on them, and that in such a case discretion was by far the better part of valour.

"Friend!" he called in his startled panic.

There was some excuse for the poor fellow, for there is nothing more calculated to make men jumpy than night marching in the desert.

Fortunately, the rest of the advance guard kept their heads, or the result might have been regrettable, since there is nothing in all the world quite so contagious as panic, even among the best of troops.

Brits advanced as far as the Gamikaub River and halted there to await news of the fate which had attended the enterprise entrusted to Myburgh and Manie Botha. General Botha himself had accompanied the latter as far as Otjimbingwe, which had been occupied almost without resistance, and then worked back with his bodyguard to Pot Mine, which was actually occupied by the general himself and the staff, accompanied only by a detachment of the bodyguard of South African police, a few hours after the Germans had left it. The intention had been that it should be occupied by a burgher force some hours before the general was due to arrive, but something had gone wrong with the time-table, and the force detailed for the work arrived to find that G.H.Q. had been installed for some hours. If the Germans had not been in such a tremendous hurry to save their skins they might quite easily have bagged the commander-in-chief with the whole of the personal and general staffs.

As a matter of fact, the general took a great many personal risks that at times caused his personal staff some little anxiety. When operations of any importance were in progress he always insisted in seeing things for himself, even though the seeing of them meant incurring a good deal of personal danger. I heard a rather amusing story apropos of this tendency of the general to running such risks. While headquarters was at Pot Mine, General Smuts arrived from the south to confer with the general officer commanding-in-chief, and apparently someone had told him of the way the general exposed himself under fire in the fight at Riet.

Smuts sent for Major Trew, commanding the bodyguard, and told him he ought not to let the general run himself into unnecessary danger. Trew replied that he had done his best to dissuade the general from going into dangerous places, but that Botha had insisted on going his own way.

"You should exercise your authority as commander of the bodyguard," said Smuts, "and not allow him to expose himself needlessly."

"That's all very well, sir," Trew replied, "but will you tell me what I am to do when the general officer commanding-in-chief tells me to go to hell?"

I never heard that General Smuts was able to supply a satisfactory answer to the conundrum.

To return to the course of the operations. It was believed that the enemy had prepared a strong position at Kubas, on the narrow-gauge line that at one time worked direct between Swakopmund and Karibib. Lemmer, with the 1st Mounted Brigade, was sent to reconnoitre this position. He found that under the threat from the south the enemy had evacuated it, and he occupied it on May 2nd. The position itself was a strong one, and had we been compelled to take it by direct assault would have . entailed considerable delay and, in all probability, a heavy casualty bill. That in miniature is the story of the whole of the operations which ended in the capture by Botha's forces of the two most important towns in South-West Africa. The enemy prepared at the cost of colossal labour position after position in a country of vast defensive possibilities, out of every one of which he was manoeuvred by the superior strategy of the Boer general.

On the same day that Kubas was occupied news came through that Manie Botha and Myburgh had succeeded in cutting the railway, and had, moreover, occupied the enemy artillery headquarters at Johann Albrechtshohe. All the guns and stores, however, had been removed by the Germans, so that the capture was more valuable for moral than for material effect. On receipt of the news, General Botha proceeded with the 1st and 2nd Mounted Brigades, the Transvaal Horse Artillery, and two of the heavy guns, and made straight for Karibib, Wylie's infantry being ordered to follow the railway through Kubas and Abbabis to the same objective.

The mounted troops arrived within sight of Karibib towards noon of the same day. May 5th, and a flag of truce was sent in demanding the surrender of the town. During the afternoon the flag returned, with a message from the *burgomaster* to the effect that the entry of the British would not be opposed. The place was accordingly formally occupied by General Brits, the German garrison having retired as soon as the Union troops were seen to be approaching. There was actually an exchange of shots between some of our advanced patrols and the German rearguard, but, contrary to every expectation, there was nothing which, by the wildest stretch of imagination, could be called an attempt to dispute possession of the most important railway centre in the colony. Most of the engines and rolling stock for the narrow-gauge line were taken by the Germans in their retirement, but we captured a large quantity of the metre-gauge stock which had been employed in the traffic between Karibib and Windhuk and on the line to the coast at Lüderitzbucht.

Practically the whole of the civilian population of both sexes had remained in Karibib. Fortunately, the Germans had left them fairly well supplied with food—they had two months' supply—or there would have been no alternative but to deport them all, since the transport problem was acute, and for a time our own troops in Karibib were on the verge of actual starvation. This was in no way due to any want of prevision on the part of those responsible for supply and transport services, but was consequent on the. unexpected rapidity with which the first objective of the campaign had been attained. Bear in mind that it was only a week since the real beginning of the forward move, and, without fighting a battle, the enemy had been forced to give up half a dozen prepared positions and retire with frenzied haste to avoid annihilation. More than all, he had lost the principal means of keeping his vital railway communications going, since he had been forced to give up the valuable workshops at Karibib on the broad-gauge line, and by the left column under Skinner, had been ejected from Usakos, where the railway works of the two-foot gauge Otavi line were situated.

It was not many days, by the way, before the Hun population of Karibib realised that British occupation of a conquered town was a different matter from the German occupation of, for example, Louvain, and set out to make hay while the sun shone. One thing there never seemed to be any dearth of in the country, and that was beer. Not that our own people ever saw any. But there were lots of it in German possession. Every enemy camp we occupied, every place in which a German patrol had halted for an hour, had its quota of empty beer bottles. Where any number of them had stayed for a night, the number of empties left behind was a positive insult to people who had nothing to drink but the brackish water of the country, and too often not much of that.

There was some quantity of beer in Karibib, and this was offered to the troops by rapacious Huns at eight shillings a bottle! It found ready purchasers even at that price. Boer tobacco, too, was sold by these harpies at four shillings a bag, the normal price of which was as many pence. There was very little to criticise, were one inclined, in the conduct of the campaign from first to last, but I certainly think an error was made in the too lenient treatment of enemy civilians, and in their being allowed to demand and obtain the extortionate prices that ruled in Karibib during a time when the troops were in a state of semi-starvation.

CHAPTER 7

Capture of Windhuk and After

The fall of Karibib and the retirement of the whole of the German field army towards the north had made Windhuk, the capital, an easy prize, which it was only necessary to reach out for to obtain. As a matter of fact, the negotiations which led up to its surrender were pleasantly conducted over the telephone from Karibib. An assurance having been given by the *burgomaster* that the entry of the Union troops would not be opposed, General Botha himself set out with an escort in motorcars on May 10th, receiving the formal surrender on the 12th. At the time of the surrender the total white population of Windhuk amounted to something over three thousand, including refugees from other places. The town was placed under martial law, but the inhabitants were informed at the same time that so long as they observed the not very onerous regulations imposed there would be no interference with their personal liberties.

With the capture of Windhuk the chief objective of the campaign was attained. This was the great wireless station which had been erected there by the Germans, with its great 800-foot high masts and mile-long aerials. According to the wireless experts, this was the second largest station in the world. I believe the German station at Norddeich ranks first in power, with Windhuk second, and our own Cornish station at Poldhu an indifferent third. Needless almost to say, the Germans had completely disabled the station by the removal of essential parts of the machinery and instruments and by pulling down the aerials. The parts they removed were irreplaceable, and it was quite impossible to get the installation working again. I am not sure that even now it has been got into working order.

Undoubtedly the Windhuk wireless was an outstanding example of the methodical way the Hun had set out to accomplish his self-

44

imposed task of bidding for world dominion. While we had been busy talking about a chain of wireless stations to encircle the globe—and doing very little but talk,—the German had built himself a station down here in the middle of South-West Africa which was capable of talking direct to Berlin! I did not see the station journals which fell into the hands of the Union troops, but I believe they actually recorded messages that had passed between Windhuk and New York. However that may be, the station was certainly in constant communication with Berlin right up to the time it became necessary for its owners to dismantle it.

Another surprise—though it ought not to have been anything of the sort, in the light of our experience of German methods of making war—was the discovery in the government laboratories of a regular poison factory, intended for our especial benefit. A number of large sealed jars attracted attention, and these, when opened and examined by a bacteriologist, turned out to be the incubators for the filthiest kind of cultures which our kindly enemy acknowledged were to have been used to infect our probable camping-grounds. In all human probability the rapidity of the movements, which had resulted so happily in the capture of the enemy's principal towns within sixteen days of their initiation, saved the invading army from falling victim to this bestial manifestation of German *kultur*. As it was, the Windhuk garrison had to get out in such a hurry to save themselves from being hopelessly cut off from the North, that they were compelled to leave this typically-*kultured* accessory to civilised war.

The campaign in German South-West Africa is merged to such an extent in the greater issues of the war that it simply cannot be viewed in its real perspective now. I have already recorded that all the work of clearing the more important half of the country, capturing the enemy's capital, and driving his field army helter-skelter to the north of the colony, was accomplished in a mere sixteen days. On the face of it, this argues that the task of the Union army of invasion had been, so far, surpassingly easy. All these great results had been achieved, too, practically without fighting.

The only important actions during this part of the campaign were Skinner's fight at Trekkopjes and a smart little affair to the east of Windhuk, in which Mentz's mounted troops scored an important success in the capture of an enemy supply column and about a hundred prisoners. I agree that it does seem rather easygoing, but, to use the words employed by Botha himself, in a general order to the troops issued at Karibib:

> The work ... has been performed under conditions which only those who have experienced them can properly appreciate.

I have seen a good many platitudinous "General Orders" issued in various campaigns. The soldier has not much to make him feel that life on active service is an unalloyed joy. Ill paid, as a rule, exposed to hardship and danger of every kind, it is often necessary to keep him in good fettle by telling him what a magnificent fellow he really is; and the more successful in turning phrases conveying the sentiment the general happens to be the more he can get out of his troops. Flattery is a good medicine in every walk of life, and it is by no means at its lowest value in war. But if ever troops did deserve all and more than was said to them about their achievements it was this wonderful army of Botha's.

That it did not fight more than it did was the fault of the enemy, who did not wait to be hit, but hustled away north at every threat. In justice to the Germans, let it be once more recorded that they were willing enough to put up a square fight if they had been given anything like a chance of engaging with a fair prospect of success. But they were up against a general of the first order, with the added disability that they were outnumbered in the field. But if Botha's army had little opportunity so far of measuring itself against the enemy in the field, at least it was given every chance of showing that it could move rapidly and take chances.

Some of the chances that were taken were enough to raise the hair of any officer not trained in the guerilla school of war, but the justification of them was that they always came off as they were intended. Take, for example, the dash of Manie Botha and Myburgh on the railway to the east of Karibib. The two brigades marched the best part of a hundred miles in three days, through waterless country, cut the railway as intended, and then went off "*into the blue*" for another eight days of strenuous marching, and that on a few strips of *biltong* which the men carried in their pockets. For eight days these men lived on what fresh meat and game they could pick up by the wayside, cooked without salt, for they had exhausted the very limited amount of rations carried in the first two days of the dash for Wilhelmstahl.

The horses had to subsist as best they could, grazing a little on such sparse desert vegetation as might occasionally be encountered. And their experience was that of the rest of the mounted troops—they went out and did, as a matter of course, the apparently impossible, though it must be said that the wastage of horseflesh was terrible. They were simply wonderful, these *burghers*. Why the Boers were able to keep the field for so long against overwhelming numbers in the Anglo-Boer war is no mystery to anyone who saw their work in German South-West Africa.

Up to this point the infantry had not had a show. The speed of Botha's movements and the turn the campaign had taken had made it entirely an affair for the mounted men. Later the infantry were to prove what they could do in the way of marching, and were to demonstrate that the South African infantryman was at least the equal of his mounted compatriot in the quality of endurance and capacity for hard work in the most appalling circumstances of country, climate and food. But the story of the great march of the infantry, which was as fine a feat of war of its kind as has ever been performed by troops, belongs to another chapter.

On the day after the occupation of Windhuk a flag of truce came into Karibib, conveying a request from Dr. Seitz, the German governor of the colony, for a meeting with General Botha for the purpose of discussing an arrangement for suspension of hostilities. Some days were consumed in correspondence between the general and the German headquarters, which had been withdrawn by the time to Omaruru, but finally a forty-eight hours' armistice, beginning at noon on the 20th May, was agreed upon.

General Botha and his staff motored out to Giftkop, which is about thirty miles north of Karibib, and there met Dr. Seitz and Colonel Franke. The conference took place under the shade of a thorn tree—not in a tent, as has been stated in some of the really dramatic attempts that have been made to describe the event. Seitz and Franke had come prepared with a set of terms that certainly did not err on the side of undue modesty. In fact, when the position of the Germans at the time is considered, one can only imagine that they thought they were about to deal with a singularly weak commander, or alternatively that they seriously thought that relief from the sea was likely to reach them before long, and intended to manoeuvre for position.

Let us regard for a moment what that position was. They had been defeated in the field and swept completely out of more than half the colony—and that the most valuable half. All their seaports and some three-fourths of the railway communications had been lost. They were cut off absolutely from all communication with the outside world, save through Portuguese West Africa, where the Portuguese were by no means well disposed to them, owing to the highhanded action of the Germans on the border. Their stocks of food and munitions of war were getting low, and the reservists, who formed the bulk of the German field force, were badly reduced in moral and anxious to see an end to the fighting. Clearly, history could hardly have blamed the German command if it had acknowledged the hopelessness of continuing the campaign and surrendered on any reasonable terms that might have been offered.

But the attitude of the governor was rather that of a conqueror than the responsible head of a government which was hopelessly defeated. He tacitly admitted that the Union troops were in effective occupation of a considerable area of the German possessions, and was good enough to say that he would agree to a continued occupation of the conquered territory—pending the return and the payment of compensation when the Allies were thoroughly beaten in Europe. A neutral zone was to be defined, north of which the Germans were to continue possession—south of it we might carry on under the limitations of tenure already noted.

Botha heard the amazing proposals quietly, and then remarked, almost casually: "My terms are unconditional surrender."

Dr. Seitz blustered about his representing an unconquerable nation of seventy millions of *kultured* people, and demanded to be told what he was to say to his All-Highest *Kaiser* if he gave up the contest without terms, but his hate exhibition was met again by the quiet statement that the only terms the general had to offer were those of unconditional surrender. The conference broke up, and it was announced that hostilities would be resumed at the expiration of the period originally announced.

It will be necessary now to hark back and follow the doings of Colonel Skinner and his brigade, with which my own unit was intimately associated.

CHAPTER 8

The Railway Advance

While the events described were taking place, Colonel Skinner had been pushing on with the task of reconstructing the Otavi Railway, which formed the left flank of the advance. Under the German regime this line was a two-foot gauge affair, which had been constructed mainly for the conveyance to the coast of the produce of the Otavi copper mines. Subsequently it was purchased by the government, and by them leased to the Otavi Company. When the advance was decided upon, it was determined to rebuild this line with the standard Cape gauge of three feet, and so make the whole system uniform throughout the colony. In this the enemy helped us materially, by tearing up the line bodily and tumbling rails, sleepers and everything down the embankment, thus leaving our own engineers nothing to do but to lay the new material down in place of that so very obligingly removed. Later the Germans got to know what was being done, and contented themselves with blowing up bridges and culverts, leaving the line in situ for us to remove for ourselves.

Our rate of advance, being determined by the progress of railway construction, was necessarily slow, and the work became horribly monotonous. Nothing but ceaseless patrol work, up and down the railway, varied by reconnaissance of the country in front kept us from absolute boredom. It was exceedingly valuable work, however, since it taught us all we wanted to know about getting the heavy cars through the bad country, and by the time the real advance began we had come to regard nothing that the country could produce as being impossible for us to manoeuvre in.

It has been mentioned already that the armoured cars bore no small part in deciding the issue of the German attack on Trekkopjes, and that they did not do even better than they did was due to the

49

want of experience of officers and men of handling them in the heavy sand. Time after time the cars stuck in the drifts and river beds while manoeuvring for position, and had to be manhandled out of their difficulties, our only casualties being sustained while thus employed. A month later we should have regarded Trekkopjes as almost ideal manoeuvring ground.

As an example of how we progressively learnt the art of getting about, and of how difficulties disappeared with experience, I was ordered one day while we were still at Trekkopjes to send a half-section—two cars—towards Ebony to ascertain if the German post there could be drawn. The cars returned in about four hours, the officer I had sent in charge reporting that it was impossible to proceed beyond Karub. Next day I secured permission to try again, and went out myself, sending an officer and a motorcyclist patrol on ahead to reconnoitre the road and report whether anything he considered insurmountable without assistance should be encountered. Three miles out we came to a river-bed about two hundred yards across, which had turned back the cars on the previous day. I went forward to examine it, and found the sand almost knee-deep. However, I thought that the worst that could happen was that the first car would stick and have to be hauled out by mule-power, so determined to risk the crossing. To our surprise the car, well driven, came through without much trouble, so we took the other through also without too much in the way of manhandling.

Karub we reached without any more trouble, but a mile farther on we came to another dry water-course, with a rocky dip into it of about one in three. I could not quite make up my mind whether to try it or not, and signalled back to Nalder to come up and look at it. Apparently the signal was understood to mean that the cars were to cross, for the next thing I saw was the leading car coming full speed at it. I could not stop them, or there would have been a mix-up between the cars, and with a plunge that threw everything into the air that was not lashed or strapped fast, the leader took the dip, ploughed through the sand, throwing it up in front like the bow-wave of a destroyer, and rocked and plunged herself up the opposite bank. We had learnt something already.

Three miles from Ebony I stopped the ears behind some rising ground, and went forward intent on climbing to the top of a low *kopje*, to see whether I could get a look at Ebony itself. A hundred yards from where we had stopped was my motorcyclist patrol, halted while one of the men repaired a puncture.

To the officer in charge I said: "Well, what about getting the cars up here? Do you think we can manage the road?"

I was vastly amused when he said: "I don't think it's possible unless they give us mules to help through the worst places."

He looked at me with more than a little suspicion when I told him that the cars were actually within a stone's throw of him at that moment, and without mules, too.

The cars were fitted with detachable running-boards for getting through bad places, but these we found quite useless for the sand, because of their tendency to turn over. Moreover, it was impossible for the drivers to keep the wheels on them, owing to the restricted view through the armoured shutter in front. Various ideas for combating the sand difficulty had been suggested. Wire netting to be laid on the sand was one which, I believe, has been adopted successfully with light cars. It was out of court in our case, since for one thing there was no netting available, and if there had been it was too heavy and occupied too much room for us.

Matting was another, and this we tried experimentally, but it was not successful, as the driving wheels simply drew it under them and threw it out behind the car. We tried thin poles, dropped between the twin tyres of the back wheels. These were good, but broke up too quickly. Iron piping was better, but this crushed out of shape and soon became useless. Finally we managed to secure a lot of two-inch angle iron, which I had cut into eight-foot lengths, with a short length of wire rope and a toggle spliced into one end. Each car carried four of these, so that when it encountered heavy sand one of these angle irons was dropped between each of the twin driving wheels. Then, as soon as the car had mounted the first one, another was dropped in front, and, when she was clear of the first, one of the crew dragged it clear of the sand, ran forward with it, and dropped it in the track again.

Thus the car had a practically continuous railway on which to run, and the heaviest sand could be negotiated at surprising speed. Where the river beds were wide it sometimes paid to lay all our irons down in advance, but the shorter stretches were better crossed by working each car "on its own." It was often murderous work for the crews, in a shade temperature of a hundred degrees, but nobody groused about that. We had to get there, and it was the easiest and quickest way of getting there we could devise.

On the 1st of May we moved camp to Karub, which was a far better site and very much superior to Trekkopjes in defensive capabilities. If only the enemy had made up his mind to repeat his experiment of attacking the brigade be must have fared a great deal worse than when he so nearly succeeded in the Trekkopjes enterprise. But the German resistance was beginning to fail under the pressure of the main advance up the Swakop, and we were to see nothing of the foe for some time to come. On the 4th the Imperial Light Horse and one section of cars were ordered to make a demonstration against Great Aukas, about half way between Ebony and Usakos, the orders being that Aukas was to be reached by the mounted troops.

The infantry and guns, with a section of armoured cars, were to advance to Ebony to cover the mounted men in case of their being opposed in force. We had our first experience of working with the cavalry on this occasion, and although the enemy decided that he was "too proud to fight," and we were thus denied the satisfaction of a heart-to-heart talk with him to compensate for the strenuous day's work, we got some value out of the operations, since we learnt that we could move in the difficult country at least as fast as mounted men. At the end of the day we returned to camp at Karub, where we were to remain until after the abortive armistice of the 20th.

The interval was by no means an idle one. After the fall of Karibib, Usakos was occupied by a squadron of the Imperial Light Horse and one section of cars. Here again we learnt something worth knowing, and that was that if we were going to keep up, we should have to look to our water supplies as carefully as to our petrol. Our average consumption of the latter worked out at about four miles to the gallon, as compared with an average on English roads of, roughly, nine miles. That was not so bad, but when we found that our water consumption was also four miles to the gallon in a practically waterless country, the problem of transport began to look alarming. There are three roads between Ebony and Usakos—and all of them bad. Whichever may be chosen—we tried all three—there are stretches of from a mile to three miles over which it is necessary to manhandle the cars even on fairly steep down grades.

The sand for mile after mile is like nothing I have ever encountered anywhere else, even when there are no river beds to add to its depth and stickiness. Three miles from Usakos the Kahn River is crossed, and no matter which road you happen to be on, there are three miles id hard pushing to be done. Even the light touring-cars have to be assisted through it. The consequence is that the twenty miles between the two places have to be covered on the first speed practically the whole way, and radiators boil dry in no time. Here is not a drop of water to be had on the road, and so, in addition to everything else, it is necessary to carry water for every contingency. This is no slight matter in a country where it is impossible to load transport vehicles to more than half normal load.

At the conclusion of the armistice the brigade moved on to Ebony, a place of unhappy memory. The Germans had a station there, probably because of the proximity of the Palgrave copper mine. There could have been no other reason for planting a station in such a spot. Ebony is not a bad defensive position, but there its charms end. A waste of barren, sun-scorched rock ridges, infested by scorpions and alive with flies, I should say it is about the worst place in the worst part of Africa. I heard it well summed up by a Rhodesian officer, who said: "If I owned Ebony and Hell, I'd let Ebony."

The ground was so hard it was impossible to drive in even steel tent-pegs, so our tent guys had to be made fast to rocks. The open ridges were exposed to every wind that blew, and very few nights passed without half the tents being blown down. To add to the discomfort of things, we were now getting up into the higher altitudes, so that while the days were like an earnest of the nether regions, the nights were bitterly cold. Fortunately we were not kept at Ebony very long, and in about a week the whole brigade, less two companies of Rhodesians left as a post, was moved on to Usakos.

Usakos was like paradise after the desert. It is really a very pretty little town, with well laid-out streets lined with pepper trees, and with a good water supply. The Germans had disabled all the pumping machinery, but this was soon put in working order by the engineers, and for the first time since landing in the country we were able to indulge in the luxury of unlimited baths. It was here that the railway works of the Otavi line were situated. Before the Germans left, the works must have been a model organisation. They had a plant of machine tools that would not have done discredit to a big engineering works in Europe, and must have been equal to anything up to the building of locomotives. It was too much to expect them to have left things intact, but the German administration evidently believed that their evacuation of Usakos would be a merely temporary affair, and that they would want the works again for their own purposes.

Nothing had been destroyed, but the essential parts of the machine tools had been removed, and many of the small tools taken up country. The drawing office, with all the plans and drawings of the railway bridges, was intact. The electric lighting installation had not been interfered with, except for the disabling of the engines, so that we were able to get it going by coupling up the dynamos to the engine of one of the mobile units of the Searchlight Section.

CHAPTER 9

Preparing for the Final Advance

The occupation of Usakos marked the end of the preliminary operations so far as the 3rd Infantry Brigade was concerned. The breakdown of the negotiations for surrender had made it evident that we should have to pursue the enemy northwards, certainly as far as Otavi and Grootfontein, to which latter place the seat of civil government had been removed, and quite possibly to the border of Portuguese West Africa. This meant a march of 250 to 400 miles into country practically unknown to the Union Staff, the only certainties being that there was little water for the first 160 miles and no supplies of any kind save a few head of cattle and some small number of sheep on the farms, if the Germans had not driven all their stock away in their retirement.

Obviously, it would have been the veriest folly to depend upon the country for anything at all. It is equally obvious that to provide for a large force in such a country as we were about to traverse meant a great deal of careful organisation, particularly when it is remembered that there was only a single line of railway over which supplies could be carried and that it was believed that the country was such that motor transport could not be relied upon. The difficulties of supplying a rapidly moving force by means of animal transport were manifestly so great that no reliance was to be placed upon it. Therefore, the one course to be taken was to make the final campaign quick and decisive when once the forward move was begun. But to ensure the certainty of a favourable result, everything down to the last detail must be perfectly organised in advance; the slightest failure or omission might well prove fatal to the whole scheme of things.

A complete reorganisation of the whole force was decided upon, and to that end the infantry of the Central Force, which had been set free by the fall of Windhuk and the success of the operations against the Germans in the South, was brought up to Walfish to take part in the closing act of the drama. The 3rd Brigade practically disappeared, the Kimberleys and Rhodesians being posted to a new 1st Infantry Brigade, made up of these two fine battalions, together with the 1st Transvaal Scottish, the Pretoria Regiment, and the 1st Durban Light Infantry. Colonel Skinner was promoted Brigadier-General and appointed to command lines of communication, and Brigadier-General Beves was given command of the 1st Brigade.

At first we were afraid that the armoured cars were to be employed on lines of communication, the country in front not being considered suitable for them to manoeuvre in. We were told the most appalling stories of what this country was like. A few miles farther on, so it was said, the ground became rocky, and there was only a single boulder-strewn track, which even a light car could scarcely negotiate. Farther north, one reached the thorn country, which was an impenetrable mass of "wait-a-bit" bush, which would effectually stop us even if we managed to get so far. But we had heard so much of the country, and had found all the information so utterly wide of the truth, that we decided to suspend judgment for the future until we had seen it for ourselves. In the meantime there was no news of what was to happen to us. At last I got permission to proceed to Karibib with a view to finding out what the dispositions were likely to be and, incidentally, to see for myself what we had to expect in the way of roads to the north of Usakos.

The first attempt to reach Karibib I don't think I shall forget for a very long time. Accompanied by my medical officer, McMullen—he has since gained the Distinguished Service Cross in East Africa—I set out early on June 10th, intending to make the double journey of forty miles in the day. The "road" was simply awful. For the first couple of miles the going was as good as we had had anywhere, which was not saying much, but then it changed greatly for the worse. The surface was either rocky outcrops, which reminded one of the very worst Belgian *pavé* ten times exaggerated, or else heavy sand, which meant severe manual labour to push the car through. Exactly half-way the car decided that it did not want to go to Karibib that day, and stripped the driving dogs of one of the rear hubs while we were trying to coax it through a sand-drift. It was of no use to try a temporary repair. There was nothing for it but to walk the nine miles back to Usakos and send out for the car next day.

So the doctor and I set out to make the best of it. We had a little water in our water-bottles—we had nearly emptied them in the intervals of pushing the car through the sand—and nothing to eat, while the sun was diabolically hot. Added to this, we knew that the enemy's patrols were in the neighbourhood and might drop down on us at any moment. A mere nine miles' walk does not sound anything out of the way, but when one is nearly exhausted by severe physical exertion, and condemned to carry forty pounds of arms and equipment under a tropical sun through heavy sand, there does not seem to be much humour in life. The return to Usakos occupied nearly four hours of the hardest walking I have ever done in my life, and we arrived "home" in the middle of the afternoon, having had rather more than enough of it.

Next day I essayed the journey with more success, and arrived in Karibib in a couple of hours from the time of starting. Things there did not presage an early advance. To say that a state of virtual famine existed does not exceed the truth. Everyone was on the shortest of short rations. Even the hospitals were living from hand to mouth. The nursing sisters had been living for days on ration biscuit and a little sugarless tea, and with hardly any prospect of better conditions in the immediate future. At G.H.Q. things were just as bad, and it was put pretty bluntly that new arrivals were not at all welcome under the existing conditions. I had known how matters stood, and had therefore brought along in the car a few supplies that made all the difference in the way I was regarded by the headquarters' mess, and made me quite popular for the time being.

At this time Karibib was occupied by a considerable force, and the only way in which supplies could be got to them was up the Otavi line *via* Usakos. It has already been recorded that this line was being relaid with the metre gauge. This had been carried as far as Ebony, and everything came to that point on the broad-gauge line. There it had to be transferred by hand to the narrow-gauge railway.

Three miles on the Karibib side of Usakos the Germans had blown up a big girder bridge, and while repairs were being made to this all the supply trucks had to be hauled by mule teams by way of a deviation that the engineers had constructed through the sandy river-bed below, and made up into trains on the other side. Add to this that engines were few, and most of those we had were suffering from boiler trouble, consequent on the use of the water from the Swakop Valley, and some idea of the difficulty of feeding the Karibib force may be gained.

Everybody was quite cheerful about it, however, and perfectly content to put up with worse in view of the promise of an early advance. The problem of the latter was entirely one of how soon the engineers could establish adequate communication with the coast, because this line, which was the source of all the trouble in Karibib, was the one link by which the advancing army could be fed and supplied. If this broke down there could be nothing for it but failure of the great enterprise, with its corollary of a retreat, and time wasted in yet another period of reorganisation and preparation for a second offensive.

Therefore, there could be no question of any forward movement until our communications had been secured, and the principal topic in every mess of the army was the progress of the railway. Even the wireless news from Europe was dwarfed into comparative insignificance, and the question of whether the Dardanelles would be forced or not took second place to the probable date of the linking up of through communication between Karibib and Swakopmund.

There was an additional reason for anxiety, in that until the advance could begin our communications were seriously open to attack, if the enemy were disposed to manifest the least enterprise. Blockhouses had been constructed, all the important bridges were held by strong detachments, and the line was patrolled, but even so it was particularly open to attack by an enemy who knew his business and was determined to stave off the evil day for as long as possible. He did not attack it until a week before the end of the campaign, but why no attempt was made, especially on the vulnerable section between Ebony and Usakos, which for weeks presented the thoroughly unsound military proposition of a line of communication which was at the same time our front, will remain one of the mysteries of an extraordinary campaign.

I have described the communications situation as militarily unsound. Therefore, it should be said that this was due to no want of appreciation of the conditions by the Union Staff. It was a situation which was forced upon us by the conditions, and could by no possibility have been avoided. That the enemy did not take advantage of it was our good fortune, and, from his point of view, an unfortunate failure to appreciate a golden opportunity when he had it.

My visit to Karibib resulted in my being able to take back the news that we were to participate in the great advance as a unit of General Beves's 1st Infantry Brigade. I was also able to gather that the view of General Botha and the staff was that we should meet with very little opposition from the Germans until we reached Kalkfeld, a hundred miles farther up the Otavi railway. According to native and other reports, the enemy was preparing a very strong position there, and intended Kalkfeld to be the scene of his last stand.

"And," said the general, "if they stand there none of them will get away."

Usakos for the next week was a busy hive indeed, the infantry of the Central Force were arriving as fast as the railway could convey them and at the same time keep pace with the supply demands. Units were being organised and new brigades being formed for duty on lines of communication, while a complete redistribution of commands and staff was carried out. The 3rd Brigade, with which we had shared the hardships and humours of the campaign, was broken up by the drafting to the 1st Brigade of the two battalions I have already named, and then reconstituted as Lines of Communication troops under Colonel Smyth. The Imperial Light Horse left us to form part of 4th Mounted Brigade under General Lukin, D.S.O., and the two 4-in. naval guns which had been our only artillery were, like ourselves, attached to General Beves's brigade.

General Beves arrived on June 12th, and on the following day came over to inspect us. Naturally, a transfer from one command, under which one has had time to shake down and become accustomed to methods, to another which is unknown has a disquieting effect for the moment. Even general officers vary, and I had got to know and believe in General Skinner, so the pleasure of being detailed for the advance was not altogether unmixed with a feeling of regret that we were no longer to serve under our old chief. However, any misgivings we might have felt were completely dispelled by our first meeting with General Beves. He was keenness personified, and what he did not succeed in finding out about armoured cars and ourselves in the course of the afternoon he spent with us was not a matter of any great moment. He left us with the impression that we were to serve under a soldier who knew what he wanted, and would prove a splendid chief if one did what was expected, but who would show no mercy to the inefficient or the slacker.

General Beves's brigade-major, "Fatty" Jones, as he was affectionately called by his intimates, was another fine soldier, and possessed the quaintest fund of humour I have ever known. His alliterative summing up at the Aus affair with the Central Force, when the Germans fled without a fight from the strongest at all the South-West positions, passed into a classic in the force. Of course, in view of what was known of the strength of the place it was expected that there would be some very heavy fighting. The very idea acted like a tonic on the troops who had been stewing in the desert for months with nothing in the way of fighting more serious than desultory affairs with enemy patrols. The disappointment was correspondingly keen when the force reached Aus and found no one there. Somebody asked "Fatty" what he thought of it.

In a voice of concentrated bitterness Jones replied: "What do I think of it? A fitting finish to a flaming fiasco!"

Poor Jones, with whom I afterwards cemented a very close friendship, was killed in France while gallantly leading his battalion, of South African Infantry, in the attack on Delville Wood.

Up to this time the transport problem had not worried me a great deal. So far as supplies needed for immediate use were concerned, we could carry them ourselves. All the heavy stores, replacement parts and spares for the cars, with the main petrol supply which we had brought with us from England, I had sent up by rail to Usakos as opportunity offered. We had, therefore, been very comfortable and free from anxiety hitherto, because no matter what happened all our stores were somewhere within comparatively easy reach. Now, however, things were to be very different.

By the very nature of our constitution we must be a self-contained unit, depending upon no one for anything but our daily rations. Kits, stores, petrol for an indefinite period for twenty-one cars and twenty-eight motorcycles, oil, spares—all had to be carried somewhere and somehow without appealing to an already overburdened brigade transport. In addition, was the nightmare of water. I have asserted that often the water consumption of the armoured cars was equal to the petrol they consumed. The nearest reliable water supply was 150 miles away, and that meant if we were to be absolutely certain of getting there each car must have a reserve of at least thirty gallons, or about two and a half terns in all.

Then about two tons of petrol besides that carried in the tanks were to be carried to make sure of things. To add to the worry of the situation, the heavy lorry which we had regarded as one of our most precious possessions turned out to be utterly unsuited to the country and ultimately had to be left behind, and one of the light lorries broke down hopelessly while carrying a load of 4-in. ammunition. So, with a transport establishment originally laid down for service in France, and further reduced by the casualties mentioned, we had to face the prospect of a journey to the northern confines of German South-West Africa.

However, I knew that the campaign had been and would still continue to be one in which things were cut to the finest of fine points, and chances were taken which nothing could have justified but success. Clearly, then, this was a case in which we had to risk something. I decided, therefore, to cut all personal kits down to the absolute minimum, abandon all the tents, and risk something on the chances of getting sufficient water on the way. These matters being settled, we bent ourselves to the task of getting things ready for the long trek that was in front.

A week before the advance began General Botha came down to inspect the 1st and 3rd Brigades. The inspection concluded with a march past of the two brigades, headed by the armoured cars. I think that everyone had expected this part of the affair to be rather humorous, and that the cars would rattle and bump their way past the saluting base, with much clanging of armour and machinery and in any sort of order. But, on the contrary, the cars, with their powerful engines turning slowly, simply stole silently past, four abreast and in perfect alignment, their grim outlines relieved by the flaunting white ensigns which we flew on gala occasions. They made an impressive sight, and, as one of the staff remarked afterwards, "No wonder the Huns don't like the look of them."

After the inspection General Botha addressed the officers of the two brigades in Dutch, his speech being rendered into English by his military secretary. Why the general prefers to make all his public utterances in Dutch I don't know, since he has perfect command of English. His speech on this occasion was one of thanks for the past and assurance for the future. Another five or six weeks, he told us, would see the end of the German hopes of retaining even a part of the Colony. As a matter of fact, it was less than five weeks afterwards that the terms of surrender were signed and South-West Africa became a British dependency.

Roughly, the plan for the advance was that the infantry were to keep to the line of the railway. General Myburgh, with the 2nd and 3rd Mounted Brigades, was to move up from Okasisse and Wilhelmstahl and carry out an enveloping movement on the right flank. General Brits, with the 1st Mounted Brigade, was detailed for a similar movement on the left. General Manie Botha, with the 5th (Free State)

Mounted Brigade, and General Lukin's brigade of South African Mounted Rifles were to move initially with the infantry. By the middle of June preparations were well advanced, and everyone, the work of getting everything in readiness being off his mind, was consumed with impatience for the order to move. It was on the 18th that the looked-for orders came—we were to move next morning.

Chapter 10

The Beginning of the End

At dawn on June 14th the advance began which was to put an end to all the hopes of the Germans that they would be able to retain their grip on South-West Africa until the issue of the war in Europe should have finally determined its ultimate ownership. The date of the beginning of the end has been erroneously stated to have been the 18th. This, however, refers to the start of the great sweep of the Mounted Brigades—that masterly conception of strategic genius that made possible the practically bloodless victory which Botha's columns were to achieve over an enemy trained in the best schools of modern war. This aspect of the campaign will fall to be discussed in its place. For the time being we will follow the work of Beves's infantry column, which led off in the great enterprise.

The Kimberleys and the Rhodesians we knew, since they had formed a part of Skinner's Brigade, with whom our lot had been hitherto cast. The new battalions were an unknown quantity. Everyone had been too busy preparing for the last act to have time or opportunity for making new acquaintances, and, besides, the troops which now constituted the 1st Brigade had arrived in such piecemeal fashion, owing to the exigencies of railway traffic, that Usakos during the last few days had been a veritable kaleidoscope in which it was impossible to distinguish the individual components of the pattern.

So it was not until the actual day of the move that we were really able to take stock of the new units with which we were now to be associated. As being the most mobile unit of the brigade, we were to move with the rear battalion, which was the Pretoria Regiment, under the command of Lieutenant-Colonel Freeth. We had thus an excellent opportunity of judging how the various regiments shaped as they moved out on the long trail.

It must not be forgotten that the conquest of South- West Africa was carried out not by regular troops, but by volunteers whose pre-war training was essentially volunteer training of a standard which in some respects fell short of that of the average British Territorial battalions. Therefore, it may be easily imagined that the critic brought up in the hard school of regular discipline would naturally have expected to find certain military shortcomings in troops of such composition. Moreover, the British regular accepts it as an article of faith that the Colonial, be he South African, Australian or Canadian, is imbued with a misplaced—from the military point of view—spirit of sturdy independence that makes him impatient of discipline and causes his officers to be afraid of drawing the bonds sufficiently tight.

It may be that some or all of these military disabilities do exist in the case of some Colonial volunteer forces. They may exist in South Africa in times of peace. But this is certain, that I have never seen better infantry anywhere than these five battalions of South Africans who moved out of Usakos on that June morning—and I have campaigned with the infantry of every one of the great military powers and with that of some of the smaller.

It would be invidious to make distinctions—indeed, it would be impossible to draw comparisons where the fighting and marching qualities of the several battalions were so equal. Still, I cannot help recording that of the whole brigade the Pretoria Regiment and the Transvaal Scottish impressed me as being up to a very high standard indeed. As they swung out across the open square that marks the northern-most boundary of the town, it was difficult to think that these spare, hard-bitten soldiers were volunteers whose ordinary avocations were those of the peaceful civilian. They looked and carried themselves like veteran regulars who had made campaigning the business of their lives. And they were as good as they looked, not only these two crack battalions, but the whole of that wonderful infantry who were now setting out on a march that in a lesser war than this would stand out as one of the highest military achievements of its kind in all history. Of the spirit of this infantry let me interpolate one characteristic story. It carries us a little ahead of the narrative, but that does not matter.

A week after we had left Usakos, and had marched rather more than a hundred miles through country which was practically waterless and during which rations had virtually disappeared from the daily calculation, we were standing by in the grey of a bitter morning while an infantry reconnaissance went forward to investigate a position believed to be held by the enemy in force. Having nothing to do in the meantime, I was chatting with one of the officers of the squadron when a man of the Kimberleys came up and saluted.

"Have you got a doctor, sir?" he asked.

"Yes," I replied; "what's the matter?"

"Well, sir, I'd like him to give me a little Vaseline for my feet. They're a bit sore." But he made no fuss.

I sent for the doctor and asked him to do what he could. The man removed his boots and what was left of his socks. How he managed to stand, let alone walk, I don't know. His feet were so bad that the doctor told him he had better get into the ambulance—that he could not possibly go on.

"That's all right, doctor," he said. "Give me some Vaseline and a bandage and I shall be right enough."

It was none of our business to make him go sick, so the doctor dressed and bandaged the poor fellow's feet. When it was finished he pulled on his boots and started to overtake his battalion with a wave of his hand and a cheery, "So long, boys! There's going to be a scrap."

And that was the spirit of them all. When the road was hard and long; when they were called upon to do a thirty-mile march, with little water and little food, under a scorching sun; when they bivouacked without blankets, with the temperature seven or eight degrees below freezing-point, it was always the same. Give them the promise of a fight at the end and they were cheery as crickets. Like all soldiers, they groused on occasion, but they only had one real grievance. Hardship they were inured to. Extremes of heat and cold they could stand. Marching on a biscuit and a half a day, and with water enough to moisten their parched mouths, was all in the game. But they had one great ground of complaint, and deeply and bitterly did they express themselves about it—the Germans would not fight.

Most of these magnificent fellows now lie in soldiers' graves in France. It was they who, after the conclusion of the South-West campaign, hastened to form the first splendid South African force that General Lukin brought over to stand shoulder to shoulder with the men of the Motherland and of the other Dominions on the fields of France. It was in stricken Delville Wood that they wrote the page which will remain a storied and a hallowed memory so long as the South African Union and its history shall endure. And the story they wrote there was an epic one, as befitted the men of Botha's army who in this African "side-show" had shown the dour stuff of which they were made. There have been troops as good as this infantry of Beves's. But no general has ever had the supreme good fortune to command better material than these South Africans.

To return to the narrative. The first day's march was to take us to Onguati, the junction of the narrow-gauge line to Otavi with the branch to Karibib. It was a comparatively easy day, for the country was known to be clear of the enemy, and there was not a great deal of patrol work to be done, so we moved practically "on our own," my orders being to give the infantry plenty of room and simply to keep in touch with the column ahead. The day was practically devoid of interest, though towards noon great excitement was caused by the first and only rain we saw during the whole campaign. There was only enough to swear by—not enough to wet anything—but still it was rain, real rain.

Onguati is like any other place in this Heaven-forsaken land—just a shed by way of railway station and a few tumbledown native huts for the accommodation of native labourers. It lies under the shadow of the Bokberg mountains, which were somewhat of a source of anxiety to us, as it was not known whether the enemy might not be preparing a stroke under cover of their inaccessible fastnesses. By this time, though, we had almost ceased to credit him with enough enterprise to attempt anything outside of his primary operation of getting out of the way without risking a fight. We were late in getting in, and found our camping-ground occupied by half a dozen dead horses and mules. It did not need the services of a vet. to certify that they were dead—they cried the fact to high heaven for themselves. So our first job was to hitch the tow-ropes on to them and drag them out well clear of the camp.

We were now getting up into the high country, which meant bitterly cold nights, and as this was our first day's experience of travelling with kits reduced to vanishing-point and with one blanket apiece, everyone felt the cold severely, especially as the day had been exceptionally hot. The night seemed interminable, and it was a relief when at last the dawn came and it was time to prepare for another day's march. This was very much in the way of a repetition of the first, though now it was just possible that the enemy might be encountered if he should take heart of grace and determine to harry our advance before the mounted troops started to move. I had orders to remain in camp until the infantry had had a two hours' start, and then to come on with my own command and the mobile transport.

I have always regarded it as a sound maxim of war that all minor disasters happen in safe areas. That is to say, it is always when you are certain that there is no foe within striking distance, and you have allowed things to become lax, that you are jumped on with both feet by an enterprising enemy, and another regrettable incident has to be chronicled. The moral, of course, is that no portion of hostile territory is to be regarded as "safe," and that it is much better to be sure than sorry. It may be a platitude, but it is nevertheless a truism that I have seen too often neglected in war.

On the principle, therefore, of being quite certain, I always insisted on the posting of proper outposts and pickets at every halt; and even at a check, when the cars had to be assisted at bad places, motorcyclist patrols were invariably sent forward to guard against surprise attack, even in the most unlikely spot. I know I was regarded as rather a crank on this question of safety against surprise, but a somewhat lengthy experience has taught me that if you once let people get into slack habits when it does not greatly matter, they will infallibly manifest slackness when it *does* matter. Although this is by no means intended as an essay on the art of war, the interpolation may not be without value to the young officer who may chance to read it; and, besides, it may be taken in the light of an explanation by some of those who may have thought that excessive caution caused more work than they considered necessary to fall upon men who were already sufficiently burdened.

Etiro was the objective of the second day's march, and here we bivouacked on good, high ground with open country in front, over which we could have manoeuvred with ease had the Germans meant business and attacked. Here we were to remain until the situation developed on the flanks. The enemy's main forces were a short twenty miles away, at Omaruru, and it was therefore necessary to take every due precaution.

I always regard the four days we spent at Etiro as being the most miserable of the whole campaign. The weather was scorching hot, with never a breath of wind to take the edge off the sun's rays, and as soon as the short tropic twilight had merged into darkness the air became bitterly cold, and by midnight everything was covered with rime. At four o'clock the brigade stood to arms, no fires being allowed to be lighted until sunrise at about 6.30.

The misery of those two hours! Owing to the cold it was almost impossible to sleep, and one spent most of the night in trying to warm oneself by sections, as it were, until by three o'clock Nature came to the rescue and one fell off to sleep. Then at four, turn out and stand to arms! And this in thin tropical clothing! Personally, I was more unfortunate than most, as I had no overcoat, thanks to a *burgher* who apparently had thought he had more right to my "British warm" than myself. Certainly, I look back to those days at Etiro with less happy thoughts than to any other period of the whole campaign, and I think most who were there would agree with me.

As I have remarked, the reason for our comparatively long halt was to give time for the movement of the mounted troops to develop. This movement began on June 18th. Brits, with the 1st Mounted Brigade, from Karibib swooped suddenly down on Omaruru, which he occupied on the 20th with very slight resistance, the Germans retiring hurriedly northwards, removing all the rolling stock and destroying the railway bridges and culverts as they went. Brits remained at Omaruru until Manie Botha's 5th Mounted Brigade and Lukin's 4th Brigade came up. In the meantime the aeroplanes of the South African Aviation Corps under Major Wallace reconnoitred Kalkfeld, where (as I have said) the enemy was expected to make his last great stand before throwing up the sponge.

This position at Kalkfeld was a very powerful one. It consisted of two semicircular ridges of hills, the southernmost lying mainly to the east of the railway, with its convex side facing our line of advance. The northern ridge lay a mile behind the other, to the west of the line, and with its concave face looking south. According to the reports of our airmen, both positions were heavily entrenched, but no traces of occupying troops could be discerned, nor were any guns seen. Native intelligence, however, had it that the ridges were held in force, and that the Germans had at least five batteries of heavy guns in position.

How the information was gained I never heard, but it was said that the German plan was to make a feint of holding the southern ridge and to retire hurriedly as soon as our attack developed. If everything worked according to programme, we should pursue through the narrow *nek* by which the railway passed through the high ground, and would come under the concentrated fire of the guns on the farther ridge as soon as we debouched on to the open ground between. Certainly the character of the ground lent itself admirably to such a plan, and I incline to think that this was indeed the German intention, because we found later that all the ranges from the northern heights to the *nek* had been carefully marked. But I am going ahead of the narrative.

CHAPTER 11

On to Omaruru

During our stay at Etiro the engineers, by superhuman efforts, had succeeded in getting the railway through, and two days before we moved on the first train came up with welcome supplies. This was followed immediately by others, and, much to my own satisfaction, one of them brought up an officer I had sent over to Karibib before leaving Usakos to draw new clothing for the men. Three months' campaigning in such country as South-West Africa, and under the prevailing conditions, had made my people into as choice a crew of ragamuffins as I have ever seen. Indeed, the order to restrict the amount of personal kit to be carried by each man was a little superfluous in most cases.

Between wear and tear and the inevitable losses sustained in such a campaign there were very few who could have mustered more than the amount allowed. The matter of clothing had given me some anxiety, because the first essential had been to get up supplies of food, and ammunition and clothing had been the last thing that was thought of. The Union troops were better off than we were, since they had been able to make good deficiencies before the move began, while we, being an Imperial unit, had either to depend upon supplies from home or rely upon the goodwill of the Union ordnance department.

And here I would like to record our great indebtedness to the unfailing kindness of the Union authorities, who invariably went out of their way to assist us in this and in every other matter in which it was necessary to invoke their aid. Our relations with them were always happy, and the spirit that animated them ever seemed to be that we were not only companions in arms, but guests of the Union and to be treated accordingly.

Thanks to the timely arrival of kit, the men of the squadron were once more in a condition of bodily comfort, not to say decency, and we could look forward with somewhat more of content to what was to come. The arrival of supplies, too, was more than welcome, since it enabled the whole force to go forward secure against starvation for at least the first week. What was to happen after that was on the knees of the gods.

We knew that the campaign was to be a sharp one, and that the general meant to finish it in two or three weeks, if it meant the killing of every animal in the army. He was taking chances that were enough to appal a less experienced commander than himself. Here was a large army being taken literally "into the air," leaving its bases to look after themselves, cutting adrift from supplies in a country without water or roads » and depending for food on the problematical repair of a single line of railway which was being systematically destroyed by the enemy as he retired! There was no reason to think that the troops could live on the country.

As a matter of fact, the information available all pointed the other way. There was no certainty of how far we should have to pursue the enemy until he could be finally destroyed or forced to surrender. There was every element present to give pause to a general who had anything of timidity in his composition. The least miscalculation, the smallest miscarriage of plans, must have been fatal to the successful issue of the campaign. But Botha is anything but a timid commander. He knew all the risks, but he also knew the mental temperament of the Germans, and, in addition, he knew of what his own troops were capable. Therefore, he deliberately accepted the risks that a lesser soldier would have accounted insuperable, and in taking them the events prove him to have been absolutely right.

The secret of Brits's descent on Omaruru had been well kept, though there is some reason to think that the Germans knew what to expect, for they had withdrawn their main to Kalkfeld, or, at any rate, to Epako, before his brigade came within striking distance. It had at least been well kept so far as our own force was concerned. While we were at Etiro some natives came in with the intelligence that the German main body had evacuated Omaruru, leaving behind a detachment of seventy-five men. According to these natives, the German detachment sent out mounted patrols at night, and the whole force stood to arms an hour before daybreak. Then, if no alarm occurred, they fell out and made themselves comfortable in the town until evening. The natives were most positive that, except for an observation post at a farm on the outskirts of the town, no particular precautions were taken by the enemy during the day.

I thought that if this information was even approximately correct, here was a job that would suit us admirably. With six cars we ought to be able to get well within easy striking distance before daylight, and then, when the German detachment had fallen out for the day, a sudden rush into the town would probably result in the mopping up of the whole force. Having worked out the details, I went to Beves to ask permission to try it. He told me the same idea had occurred to him, and that had it been a day earlier he would have let me go. "But," he added, "other orders have come through since, and it can't be done now." The "other orders" were simply the announcement of Brits's movement!

As it turned out eventually, it was a good thing that the proposed foray did not come off, since it was a physical impossibility for it to have succeeded on account of the difficulties of the ground. Instead of being able to get to Omaruru in about three hours, as I thought we ought to do, it would have taken a day, and then, when we had got within raiding distance, it would have taken hours instead of minutes to get into the town. We might have frightened the enemy into leaving the town, but we certainly should never have got near enough to do him any material harm. Which goes to show that the best-laid plans of war may come to nothing when their authors do not, for any reason, take proper account of the nature of the ground over which they are to be carried out. As I have remarked in a previous chapter, one of our severest handicaps throughout was want of knowledge of the country.

Brits occupied Omaruru on June 20th in the early morning. All that day mounted troops and guns of Lukin's brigade streamed through Etiro on their way to consolidate Brits's gain and to set him free for his great enveloping move far out on the left. At the same time, away to the east, a similar movement was happening, the troops involved being the mounted brigades of Myburgh. Their day's objective was Giftkop, the scene of the abortive conference of a month before. From there they were to push off on the long trek that was eventually to take them to Grootfontein, the centre of the German administration and the new capital. It was to be a magnificent operation of war which was to ensure us a practically bloodless victory, but we of the infantry regarded it with mixed feelings, for we knew only too well that the probable effect would be that the enemy would abandon his central positions without fighting under the influence of the threat of complete envelopment. We had thirsted and starved, and we knew that more thirst and starvation were in front. The only compensation to be looked for was in the hope that the enemy would stand somewhere and let us do for him what he had taunted us with being unable to achieve—beat him squarely in a stand-up fight. But hope springs eternal, doesn't it?

On the morning of the 21st the infantry and heavy guns moved out before daylight. In order to let them get well on the way I was ordered to move at ten o'clock, escorting the whole of the motor transport of the brigade, as well as the heavy searchlight section, which was finding it exceedingly difficult to progress at all. Their cars were much too heavy for the country, and were greatly underpowered for the work. That they got as far as they did was extremely creditable both to the officers and the men.

For a mile or two beyond Etiro the road was quite good, and I began to think we were really about to find decent going at last. Vain hope! Presently the ground began to get rocky and the river beds more frequent and difficult to negotiate. Five miles out it became positively appalling. Heavy boulders and rocky outcrops which often meant an hour's work with pick, shovel and crowbar to enable the cars to pass; sand as heavy and deep as anything we had yet encountered; and deep *nullahs* which often meant more road making to render them negotiable, made progress very slow, and it was then that I began to see that our proposed surprise visit to Omaruru a few days before would have ended in a fiasco.

Instead of being an easy run, as we had anticipated, this was the hardest day's work we had done—worse even than the passage from Ebony to Usakos. It was getting late in the afternoon when we came in sight of Omaruru. The first building to come into view was the outpost farm, of which the natives had told us at Etiro. It had been turned into a veritable fortress by its late owners. Trenches had been dug and walls loopholed for rifle fire, and two machine-gun emplacements built. It had not been defended, however, its garrison having evacuated it as soon as Brits's troopers appeared on the skyline. We stopped to have a look round this place, in the belief that our road troubles were ended, and that we had plenty of time to spare. We did not know the approach to Omaruru itself.

Dropping down a steep descent from Outpost Farm, we found ourselves faced with an ascent on the other side of a dry river bed, with a gradient of about one in nine and sand almost up to the axles of the cars. Over two hours it took to get the cars up this ascent of little more than a quarter of a mile in length, and by the time they were all up everyone was nearly dead beat. We proceeded to form camp on the top of the hill, and looked forward to a quiet night to compensate for the labours of the day. Something done had earned repose.

Omaruru is certainly one of the prettiest towns in South-West Africa—not that that is saying very much, but one comes to regard anything that is green as being a veritable oasis of beauty in such a land. It lies down in the bed of the Omaruru River, and is well timbered and has a plentiful water supply. It was here we had our first sight of running water. Not that there was much running about it, for the river was reduced to a mere trickle through a wilderness of sand, but it was real water and it was actually flowing. I think every soul in the column, from the brigadier downwards, walked down to the river to see the curious and unwonted spectacle of water trickling along a sandy channel.

The three-span bridge by which the railway crosses the river had been partially destroyed, but otherwise everything in the place was intact, and very few of the inhabitants seemed to have left. There were several hundred civilians of both sexes in the town, and from their demeanour they did not appear to concern themselves much about the change in the ownership of the country. They were well treated by the troops, and, after the manner of these people, they were not long in starting to make money out of their conquerors. Chickens and eggs were fairly abundant, and there was some supply of fresh milk—something we had not seen up to then.

It had been reported in Karibib that Colonel Franke was at loggerheads with the civil elements in the German councils. The latter, it was said, wanted to surrender. The end was inevitable, they held, and no good purpose could be served by prolonging the campaign. Besides, they argued, the British occupation would be a mere temporary inconvenience. As soon as the war in Europe was settled—and it could only end in the one way—they would get back their colony and a round sum by way of indemnity. Franke's answer to this was that he was a soldier, whose orders were to hold out to the uttermost and to keep a large force of hostile troops engaged, and thus prevent the possibility of their being sent round to assist in the conquest of East Africa.

Franke is stated to have gone even farther, and to have said that when resistance became hopeless he would retire with his regulars through the Caprivi Strip, at the north-eastern corner of the colony, and endeavour to make his away across the continent to join hand, with the Germans in East Africa. It had been currently reported that Franke had had constructed certain large flat-bottomed boats which were to be used for the crossing of the Kunene River in the projected breakaway. The feasibility of the plan had been much discussed by us, and opinions were greatly at variance as to whether a large body of men stood any chance of being able to accomplish such a journey.

Some held that the idea was so utterly futile that a soldier of Franke's calibre would never have entertained it, and laughed to scorn the story of the boats. Others again were of opinion that the enterprise stood at least a sporting chance of success, and was therefore justifiable in its inception. The truth of the story became apparent at Omaruru, for alongside the railway lay six fifty-foot surf-boats which could have been intended for nothing else than the flight across Africa.

Why they had been abandoned there I do not profess to know. Possibly now that the time was drawing near Franke was better able to appreciate the difficulties of his project, and decided that even a South African internment camp would be preferable. On the other hand, it is possible that the suddenness of Botha's advance took the Germans by surprise, and they were forced to abandon the boats. I am rather inclined to believe in the former theory, for the reason that had Franke seriously intended to persist in his first plan the boats would never have been taken off the railway trucks at Omaruru. The obvious thing to have done with them was to send them straight up to the border.

By the time we had settled down to bivouac for the night, and everyone had made himself comfortable for the time being, it was nearly dark. We were not to be left undisturbed, however. Just as I had finished seeing everything to rights an orderly came over from brigade headquarters with a message from Beves that I was to go over and see him at once. When I arrived I found that it was a meeting of the officers commanding units of the brigade. News had come in that the enemy was in force at Epako, about fifteen miles north, and that the brigade was to attack him at eight o'clock on the following morning. The infantry were going to move at one in the morning, and we were to follow at five, so as to be in position at the appointed time.

As there was rather more than half a mile of sandy river bed to be crossed, to say nothing of the "road" itself, this meant that the ears had to be got across that night. Beves remarked that it would probably take us all night to cross, so the sooner we got about it the better. I went back to camp and gave the necessary orders, and then walked down to look at the crossing. After seeing it I thought we should be lucky if we got the armoured cars alone over that night, and decided to concentrate efforts on that and, if necessary, to let the rest follow next day. At least the fighting part of the squadron should be up in time to take part in the attack.

We had had one surprise already that day. After thinking we had passed the worst of the country we had found that German South-West Africa was like its owners—never to be depended upon from one day to another. The crossing of the Omaruru was the second surprise of the day. To walk across meant that one sank in the soft sand half-way to the knees, and it looked all Lombard Street to the proverbial china orange that to get the cars over would mean the severest kind of manual labour. As soon as the first armoured car showed up I sent it along to try the crossings and to the utter surprise of everybody she went through without a check. So did the second and the third, and to make the story short the whole squadron was across in little more than half an hour. The explanation was simply that the sand being wet, "packed" under the driving wheels and gave them a solid drive. The general came down during the evening and was more surprised than ourselves to find us across and the men camped and fed.

It was a bitterly cold night, and we blessed the men of one of the field ambulance units who had built a fire in such close proximity to a large tree that the latter had taken fire. We completed the good work by felling the tree and building other fires under the trunk until we had the best camp fire I have ever seen. Thanks to this, we slept fairly warm for the first time since leaving Usakos.

General Botha had established his headquarters in the town, so, after seeing things in order, I walked down to see the staff. They were all in high spirits at the successful development of the advance, and were hopeful, in view of the news that the enemy meant to fight at Epako, that we should get them there or at Kalkfeld.

CHAPTER 12

Chasing Our Tails

The ascent from the Omaruru leads up on to the edge of the Kalkfeld, which, as the name conveys, is a vast chalky plain. The road, of which there is but the one, is no better than those of the country nearer the sea, except that there is not so much deep sand. The difficulties are, however, enhanced by the rocky character of the ground and by the fact that the country is covered by a thick thorn scrub, which for the most part makes it impossible for cars to leave the track. On the whole, it was more suitable for our purposes than the country we had come through, which again was not saying much for it.

We left Omaruru two hours before daylight, with all our head lamps burning, and must have made an imposing sight to the citizens of the town who were early astir. The appointed rendezvous was twelve miles distant, and as we had until seven to cover it we took things fairly easily, especially as I did not want to get mixed up with infantry and guns on the line of march. Soon after daylight we met a dispatch rider on his way back to Omaruru. From him we learnt that there had been a fight at Epako the evening before, in which the S.A.M.R. had been engaged and had had a couple of men killed. He volunteered the information that the Epako position was a very strong one, and that the enemy was expected to defend it. Hearing this, I determined to push on and chance overrunning the other troops—we did not want to miss anything that might be going.

Arriving at the appointed rendezvous a little in front of time, we found that Beves had gone on with the leading battalion, leaving no orders for us. Accordingly we pushed on, passing transport, infantry and guns, until we overtook the general a mile in front of Epako. From here the position looked what it was, admirably adapted for defence, with high ridges dominating all the approaches, and with the railway winding away behind to afford every facility for retirement in case of necessity. But all was peace, perfect peace. The Germans had thought discretion the better part of valour once more. They had blown up the large two-span bridge the night before and gone off into the blue again. They could not have left many hours before we arrived, for there was a heap of still warm ashes on the line where the demolition train had stood while the bridge was blown up.

The enemy had been at some pains to improve a naturally good defensive position. The ridges were seamed by trenches and *sangars*, with emplacements for artillery and machine-guns, all excellently placed and constructed. Whatever else may be said of their conduct of the campaign, the Germans at least knew most things about military engineering. I had the opportunity of going over a number of their prepared positions, and I do not think I ever saw a badly placed trench or one that was not well engineered. They expended endless labour on the preparation of their positions, which they never seriously defended, but none of that labour was wasted supposing it had been decided to stand. The fact is that they were never given an opportunity to defend them—they were hustled out by the masterly strategy of Botha.

Apropos of this an amusing story was told of a captured German officer, who expressed his disgust at our methods in characteristic fashion. "What chance have we?" he asked. "We prepare a good position and wait for you to attack it. Then one morning we look out in front and we see *burghers*. We look to the right and we see *burghers*. To our left, *burghers*. Across the rear, more *burghers*. It isn't war, it's a hippodrome!"

The dispatch rider's story of the previous night's fight turned out to have been, like the report of Mark Twain's death, greatly exaggerated. Apparently a mounted patrol had come into collision with some of the destroyers of the bridge and shots had been exchanged, one man on our side being slightly wounded.

During the morning General Botha and his staff arrived from Omaruru, and left later, I believe, to see Brits, who was by this time well out on the left. Soon after nine o'clock Beves and Lukin came along, and told me that some of the S.A.M.R. were in action about four miles in front. They were engaged with a strong force of the enemy and had sent for support. I was told that I was to send out a section of cars, which was to leave as soon as possible, and that it was to go prepared to be out for three days.

I had made a point of always having one section ready for a jump like this, the duty being taken by each of the three sections in turn. It happened to be Nalder's turn this time, and in seven minutes by the watch he was away with six cars and eight motorcyclists. Half an hour later the two brigadiers came back, and as they were passing Beves called me over and asked when the section would be ready to leave. When I told him it had left over twenty minutes before he looked incredulous for a moment, and then remarked to Lukin: "Smart work, that!"

Epako was not at all an unpleasant place. For one thing there was a fair water supply on a near-by farm. The country was green, the South Africans voting it ideal cattle country. They were enthusiastic about the grass, but for my part I, in my ignorance, should have said that no self-respecting animal would eat it, unless under the duress of absolute starvation. The farm of which I have made mention was being run, in the absence of her husband, who was a German officer, by a very alert and vinegary lady, who strode about among the troops with a *sjambok* in her hand and an automatic pistol in her pocket.

She was full of complaints about the occupation of her farm. She objected to horses and transport animals being watered at her well, because she wanted the water for her own stock. Unable to get satisfaction from anyone else, she set off to look for General Botha himself. I believe she succeeded in seeing him, but I do not know what happened. Later in the day she dropped on me with the complaint that a soldier had taken away one of her cats. I told her I was very sorry if anything of the kind had happened, and that if she could point out the man I would see that he was dealt with. "*Ach!*" she said, "I am von voman among tausends of mens and no von vill protect me!" I have never met a woman who was more capable of looking after herself than this German Amazon.

I had another encounter with her before we left Epako. Some of my people were wandering about the country when they came across a fine yearling calf, which they promptly shot and proceeded to hang to a tree and dress. The lady came to me in a towering rage, with a strip of the skin in her hand. I went with her, and found the deceased calf already cut up into joints. There was no getting away from it—the calf was hers, and it had been killed by my own people, so I offered to pay a fair value for it. She was very abusive, and told me exactly what she thought of the British and of myself in particular, so, instead of paying cash for the animal I gave her a receipt. Whether she ever collected any money on the strength of it I never heard. I did hear that she showed my receipt to everyone who chanced to pass and that it amused them vastly.

We remained at Epako until the following morning. The infantry went forward during the night in consequence of intelligence that the Germans were in force at Otjua, a dozen miles farther north. It was the same old story. The brigade would attack at daylight—if there was any enemy to be attacked. We were to have followed on soon after dawn, but just as we were getting ready a message came back to say that the Germans had gone and there was no need to move until the afternoon. We did not move, therefore, until shortly after midday, and reached Otjua in a little more than a couple of hours. There we found Nalder and his section. They had joined up with the S. A. M. R. as instructed, and had had a smart little affair with the enemy, in which they had taken a couple of prisoners, one of whom was wounded severely.

Otjua was just a farm on the top of a hill, which at one time must have had an ample water supply, since there was a huge dam and reservoir in the valley. The natives, however, said that the supply had given out three years before, and that there was now only a very spare and irregular supply. There was certainly little enough when we arrived, and what there was was far from good.

We were now only two marches from Kalkfeld Post, where the great German stand was to be made. In two days we were to attack and, as we hoped, finally to settle the outstanding account with them. That night I went back with General Beves to Epako to see General Lukin, who was to be in command of the whole movement. While the two generals discussed the dispositions for the attack, Jones and I fell in with Sir Abe Bailey, who was acting as Lukin's brigade-major. He was doing himself quite well—he actually managed to find whiskies and soda, a thing we had not seen for weeks. And it was excellent whisky, too, as I remember. On the way back to Otjua we somehow missed the road and went on for miles, until we came in sight of the fires of the German rearguard patrols. Needless to say, we did not go on to investigate—it was near enough as it was—and we finally got back to Otjua in the early hours of the morning.

Next day the brigade moved on to Okosongora, the armoured cars, with Beves and the brigade staff on board, forming the advanced guard. Why the Germans allowed us to move through this part of the country without molestation will remain another of the mysteries of a campaign full of surprises. From here to Kalkfeld itself the country is a succession of hills and *kopjes*, every yard of which could be usefully disputed by a determined enemy who knew his business. The ground was so bad that for most of the distance it was impossible for flanking patrols to search the ridges, and here and there the road wound through *neks* in the hills that could have been easily converted into little Gibraltars. Better country for enterprising troops to hold up and harass an enemy's advance could hardly be imagined. Had the Germans elected to worry us here it might easily have taken weeks to cover the distance we actually completed in two days.

In justice to the German command, it must be remembered that the flanking movements of the mounted brigades had developed by this time, and he was getting anxious about his communications with the north, and with good reason. Still, these movements were taking place very widely on the flanks, and there is some reason to think that if he had offered determined opposition to the infantry advance he could have materially delayed the end. Desperately situated as the Germans were, I believe they ought to have tried it.

The end was certain, and it would have been less ignominious to make a real effort to break up Botha's combinations instead of allowing the Union army to perform a species of triumphal march through the country. They must have known the risks we were taking, and that, if the time-table did not work out as intended, we should be in a parlous case, and with this in view my own opinion is that they ought to have made some attempt to hold us up. I do not consider it could have succeeded, but there was at least a chance and Franke ought to have taken it.

The brigade bivouacked at Okosongora, and during the evening a *pow-wow* was held at headquarters to settle the details of the morrow's battle. Nearly everyone was certain that there was to be a battle, in spite of all our previous experiences of the enemy's fondness for the discreeter methods of war. He had been fortifying and preparing Kalkfeld for weeks past, and had announced that here or nowhere he intended to die, if need be, in the last ditch. Moreover, it was the last really strong position in the country, so there was every reason why he should stand here, and no discernible military reason why he should not, unless he intended to go over the Portuguese border and submit to be disarmed and ignominiously interned.

True, our latest aeroplane reconnaissances had failed to disclose the presence of any number of troops, but in such country it is easy to conceal large bodies of men from the inquisitive eyes of aerial observers, and all the native intelligence pointed to the fact that the Germans were really there and intended to stay until we turned them out by force.

After the *pow-wow* we fell to discussing the chances of the morrow. I made myself the least bit unpopular for the moment by offering to lay a shade of odds that the Germans would have left before we got there. The brigadier would not have it at all—he was absolutely certain that at last we were to get what we had been longing for, a real chance at the Hun. Most of the others were equally certain, but there were one or two doubters, so we stayed up well into the night discussing the prospects. On the whole, I think the "Ayes" had it. Of the glorious Battle of Kalkfeld which ensued—or, rather, did not—we will speak in another chapter.

CHAPTER 13

Kalkfeld and the Pursuit to the North

Long before daylight on June 24th the infantry moved silently from the bivouacs of Okosongora towards the Kalkfeld position. The plan of attack was, roughly, that Beves's brigade was to assault the ridges on the right with a part of the force, holding the remainder ready to push through the *nek* to the German village beyond, when the enemy had been cleared off the *kopjes* forming the first position it was believed he intended to hold. The movement was to be supported by a flanking movement of the 5th Mounted Brigade under Lukin, who was in command of the attack. Overnight it had been arranged that I was to detach one section to work with Lukin's mounted men, reporting to Beves with the other two. I was to be in position in front of Kalkfeld as soon after daylight as practicable.

From Okosongora to the appointed rendezvous the road was not at all bad. No sand was encountered, and although the track was very rough it was not so bad as to impede progress, and we were thus able to be well up to time. At the moment I made my report the Rhodesians had just begun to move forward in extended order to reconnoitre the position, while the Transvaal Scottish were moving slowly up the railway parallel with the Rhodesian line of advance. Not a shot had been fired and there was no sign of the enemy. Was it to be another disappointment?

Beves himself remarked, as I made my report, "I don't believe this position is occupied." He sent us to work in by the road through the *nek*, with orders not to get in front of the Scottish, and after we had proceeded thus for a mile and nothing had happened, I received a message from Lukin saying that we were to push on through the *nek* as far as the German police post, engage any enemy we found there, and hang on until we were supported. I was absolutely certain that the enemy had gone, so we pushed on with more speed than I should otherwise have considered safe, and in a very few minutes we were in Kalkfeld itself. The only Germans we found there were a lame man, who was installed as caretaker of a farm, six women and as many children! The man spoke very fair English, and from him I learnt that the enemy's troops had evacuated the place two days before, after blowing up the bridges on the railway.

I sent a motorcyclist back to acquaint the brigadier with the state of affairs, and a very few minutes later General Botha and the staff came in. Botha was as nearly annoyed at the turn of events as I ever saw him, but it could not be helped: the Germans had once more chosen the paths of discretion, and there was now nothing for it but to continue the pursuit, even if it took us to the Portuguese border.

Kalkfeld was a curious little place, inhabited by a curious little community. There was only one considerable house in the place except for the police barracks. This was a farmhouse which belonged to a German artillery officer. I forget his name, but he must have been a person of some consideration in Germany. The story as told to me by the lame caretaker was that his master was at one time a general staff officer in Berlin, but had got into some sort of trouble there and been compelled to come to South-West Africa. He had lived here with his wife until the latter became tired of the life and returned to Germany, the husband visiting the Fatherland every two years. As the outbreak of war came while he was on one of his periodic visits, he had not returned to Kalkfeld, and nothing was known there about him.

It was an ordinary enough story by itself, but there must have been a tragedy of some kind underlying it. Evidently the exile had kept up much of the style to which he had been used at home. Outside, the house was like any other farmhouse of its kind. Inside, it was furnished like a better-class house in Germany, with expensive carpets and pictures that would not have done discredit to the gallery of a connoisseur. The native servants wore livery—and I must say that these liveries were the one evidence of poor taste in the *ménage*. They were simple horrors in their garishness. Nothing that money could provide to minister to a life of comfort and luxury was wanting in this strange abode far up in the African desert.

We were not long in establishing friendly relations with the people. They were particularly anxious to hear our side of the European news, though it was soon apparent that they had heard all the news of the war as issued by the Germans for the consumption of their own people. One of the first questions they asked was: How many German troops were there in England, and what was the name of the general who had commanded at the capture of London? Of course, we told them that the only German troops in England were there as prisoners of war, and that as for London having been captured—well, what were we doing in Africa if England was being invaded by the Germans? That produced no effect.

I next tried another line in the effort to convince. I pointed out that if the Germans were really in England, it meant that the British navy must have been dealt with first of all. That they admitted. Very well then: with the British navy out of the way, how did it happen that we had come out from England without being molested? That was quite easy—we had only come from the Cape, and that did not mean a sea passage at all. They declined to take my word for it that we had really come from home, so I tried still another line.

I asked how long it was since they had heard from home. That was a poser, and they had to admit that it was many months since they had had letters. Triumphantly I showed them envelopes bearing the London post-mark of six weeks before, but even that brought us no nearer. The only thing that did shake them at all was when the Transvaal Scottish came in. The sight of a kilted battalion whom they took to be Highlanders carried the conviction that the English were, at any rate, so far masters of the situation that they were able to bring regulars from home to assist in the conquest of this German corner of Africa. It was curious that the tardy conviction that their own people had lied to them about the events of the war in Europe should have come as the result of an entirely erroneous presumption.

Of course, we knew that a great deal of false news had been disseminated with a view to keeping up the flagging spirits of the reservists. The newspapers published in Windhuk up to the time of its occupation were full of embroidered reports, but it was not until now that we really knew what a tremendous erection of fabricated news had been built up by the German administration. If it did little credit to their sense of truth and honesty, it at least showed that they were by no means wanting in imagination. One idea that we found pretty prevalent among the unofficial Germans was that, so far from being a victorious army, we were really a defeated force retiring in front of an avenging German army from Europe which had landed at Swakopmund!

I do not think any but the most ignorant believed it, but the story was at least an ingenious explanation of the rapidity of our movements. However that may be, it seems to argue a very low morality among the German administrators that they should have descended to such palpable deception of their own people, as well as a very low morale among the latter that it should have been necessary to buoy them up by the manufacture of what was, to use its proper appellation, a tissue of lies known by its manufacturers to be such.

We had expected to find something like a decent water supply at Kalkfeld, but with the exception of a well at the police post, which gave a limited amount of water for about two hours and then had to be left for six to refill itself, there was none. The last water had been at Otjua, two marches to the rear, and the transport animals were beginning to feel the want of it very badly. The horses of the mounted brigades out on the flanks were doing better, as they had pushed on into the cattle country, in which there is some amount of permanent water. In ordinary times water for the Kalkfeld farms had been available on the railway. At Kalkfeld station, about four miles beyond the police post, there was a well which in normal times was said to produce over 30,000 gallons a day, which was pumped up into the two large overhead filter tanks for the supply of the engines.

Before the enemy left, however, he had taken effective measures for preventing us from having the use of this well. The pumping engine had been disabled by the removal of the crank and shaft and all the valve gear, while the pump rod had been disconnected and, with the bucket, had been allowed to fall to the bottom of the well, thus irretrievably smashing it. There was another well near the station, but that did not produce enough water to supply the needs of a tithe of the force. Unfortunately, too, the main well was over 170 feet deep, and to get up that length of cylinder rod and put the machinery into order would have taken more time than could be spared.

There was nothing for it, then, but to push on to the next water, which was—somewhere in South-West Africa! The map showed "temporary" water at intervals, but we had learnt enough about these temporary water-holes to know that they were not to be relied upon for a single pint of water. Even the permanent supplies were not always what might have been expected. Very often the only "permanence" about them was that there would be perhaps twenty gallons of a semi-fluid mud at the bottom of the hole, and when this had been scooped out there would be no more until next day. Then we were never sure that even this would be fit for consumption until it had been tested for poison.

In connection with this matter of the poisoning of the water, it is fair to say that during the later phases of the campaign the Germans did not poison the wells. In the early stages there was a lot of it done, but even so, it was done openly, as it were. The poisoning generally took the shape of a bag of Cooper's sheep-dip thrown into the well, or else a few gallons of carbolic acid poured in. There was no mistaking the smell of either, so there was no excuse for anyone's drinking the stuff. Naturally, a great deal of hardship was caused by this dirty game, because of the deprivation of water it entailed on our troops, who, after a long march with a particular water-hole as the objective, would arrive to find the water undrinkable. This meant a further trek to the next water, with the strong probability that this again would be found to have been poisoned.

There were a few cases in which men were so overcome by thirst that they drank the poisoned water, but I never heard that anyone died as a result. General Botha sent a very stern warning to Franke, early in the campaign, threatening to hold the German commander personally accountable for any deaths by poison among the Union troops. The reply was characteristic, to the effect that we had not been asked to come and drink the water—it belonged to the Germans, and surely they could spoil their own water if they desired! However, the warning seemed to have produced the proper effect, for the poisoning of the water-holes ceased forthwith. All the same, we took no risks, and no standing water was allowed to be used until the chemists had passed it as fit for consumption.

After the fiasco of Kalkfeld the brigade bivouacked above the post until the next day, when the advance was resumed towards Otjiwarongo, between forty and fifty miles farther north. We were moved up to Kalkfeld station to form a guard for the aeroplanes, which were then working from there, and to follow on as soon as the 'planes moved forward. I was warned that we should probably be attacked as soon as the infantry had got well clear, as intelligence had been received that an enemy force of three mounted companies had been concentrated at Outjo, about thirty miles to the N.W., for the especial purpose of attacking and destroying the aeroplanes. I did not believe that our luck would be in to such an extent. We would have taken on three companies with all the pleasure in the world, particularly on such favourable ground as that of Kalkfeld, if only the enemy would pluck up heart of grace to try it. But although we did not expect him to do anything of the kind, I made all possible preparations for his entertainment if he did decide to call upon us, and, had he done so, I do not think he would have had any reason to complain of our remissness as hosts.

We did get an alarm one morning, when a very hot and breathless motorcyclist—not one of my own, by the way—came in from the north with the story that he had been sent back to warn me that a large force of the enemy had broken back through the S.A.M.R. and were coming down upon me. His instructions were, he said, to tell me that I must expect to be heavily attacked in a couple of hours. I felt confident that we could hold our own, but as I knew there was a company of the Rand Rifles within three or four miles on their way up to relieve me, I thought I might as well let them have a share in the day's work, and sent back a cyclist to tell them to hurry up. They arrived within the hour, closely followed by a battery of 5-inch howitzers, whose commanding officer had also heard the news and had pushed his guns along as hard as they could go in order to be sure of missing nothing. By the time all these were up I was certain that when the enemy did arrive we could attend to his requirements in quite unexpected fashion.

But it was like all the rest of these alarums and excursions in this most disappointing campaign—the report of his coming was all we ever heard of the enemy. We stood to arms for three hours, during which time I had sent out patrols to try to get touch with the Germans if they were in the neighbourhood, but they returned having seen no trace of any hostile force. It turned out eventually that the motorcyclist who had brought in the story had seen a transport column south and had assumed the rest. The reason of the apparent retirement of this column was that it had overshot the road it had been ordered to take and was coming back to find it!

While we were at Kalkfeld a detachment of prisoners came in and was handed over to me to be sent down to Omaruru. They were a mixed lot, partly Germans and partly South African rebels who had been "out" with Maritz in the rebellion. They were delivered by a *burgher* subaltern, who did not appear to be at all certain of how many there were, while as to a nominal roll of his prisoners, he had not heard of such a thing. The number he thought he ought to have tallied with the count, so he was satisfied, but I thought I ought to know more about it.

I therefore took their names, and when I came to about the sixth and said, "What is your name?"

I was astonished to get the reply in broad Scots: "Michael McDonald, sir."

I made him repeat it, and then, having made sure that my ears had not deceived me, I asked him what on earth he was doing in the *rôle* of a rebel.

"I didn't agree with the policy of the government," was his answer.

I looked significantly up at the tree under which we were standing and merely remarked, "Neither do I."

The rest of the rebels were Dutch and presumably knew no better, but I should dearly have liked to have the dealing with Mr. Michael McDonald. These prisoners seemed to be rather glad to have been taken, especially the Germans.

While we were at Kalkfeld we experienced more than one instance of German ingratitude for lenient treatment at the hands of the British. There were several farms within a radius of five miles of the spot, and where the men of the place had not accompanied the German forces in their retirement they were left, by General Botha's orders, in undisturbed possession, and, were given permits to reside on their farms. Nearly all of these men had been soldiering within the month, if appearances were anything to go upon, and had just remained behind when they realised that the game was up, trusting to British humanity and sense of justice. Whenever we had occasion to visit any of these farms the occupants made no attempt to disguise their dislike of us. At first they were even openly discourteous, but we soon stopped that by insisting that when any of our own officers called at their farms they were to be treated exactly as German officers would have been before the British occupation.

As an example of their attitude to us I will record the experience of one of my own officers at a German farm about a couple of miles away from the post. I had sent him out on some duty or other—I forget exactly what it was—and on the way back he called at the farm and asked the Hun owner for water. The latter curtly said he had no water on the farm. There were two pails of milk standing on the stoop, and, seeing them, the officer asked if they could not have a drink of that, whereupon the German kicked them over and said: "I would sooner do that with them than give a drink to a Britisher." When the matter was reported to me I went out myself to interview this engaging gentleman and made him apologise to the officer concerned, threatening that if he did not do so I would take him into Kalkfeld under arrest and put him in close confinement, permit or no permit.

Leniency seems to be completely thrown away on these people. They certainly do not practise it themselves, as witness the treatment accorded to British civilian prisoners in South-West and in East Africa. The German mind apparently is quite incapable of appreciating higher motives, and ascribes the treatment extended to their prisoners to weakness or the fear of reprisals. It is a mistake to treat them well, since it only engenders contempt for our foolishness. Moreover, it reacts unfavourably on our own people who have the ill fortune to fall into the hands of the Huns, for the reason that the latter know full well that however badly they treat our people we are certain not to come down to their level and exact an eye for an eye.

Nor would I for a moment argue that we should go to the lengths that the Germans are prepared to go, but there is a middle course between the studied brutality with which the Germans treat their civilian prisoners and the fraternal kindliness we extend to the captured Hun. The saying that in war you should only leave to the people of a conquered country eyes wherewith to weep for their losses is, doubtless, the last word in brutality. It is a maxim of war that does not, and I trust never will, find a place in our own textbooks, but in avoiding the one extreme we appear to go to the other and to make war as pleasant and profitable as possible to the enemy's civilian population.

It is a certainty that never in their lives were the civilians of the northern parts of South-West Africa so well off as under the British occupation. Not only were they allowed to carry on their avocations without interference, but they were allowed to charge their own prices for commodities and to withhold them if the troops were not willing to submit to their extortion. Toleration of that kind of thing may be magnificent ethics, but it is not war. It is not war as the German mentality visualises it.

CHAPTER 14

Nearing the End

From Kalkfeld to Otjiwarongo is about forty miles of the worst going in the country. At the best there is only a very limited supply of water anywhere along the road, and as all the wells had been reported as having been destroyed by the enemy, the probabilities pointed to a waterless trek over this desolate forty miles. There was supposed to be water at Omuranga, five miles on from Kalkfeld, the next being at Okanjande, twenty-five miles farther. In normal times there is a fairly good supply at the latter place, where the British civilian prisoners had been interned. In any case, therefore, the infantry had a thirty-mile march before reaching water, and this over a road that was worse than anything they had encountered hitherto.

In order to minimise the hardship as much as possible the first portion of the march was made during the hours of darkness, but the troops suffered almost as much from the cold at night as they would have done from heat and thirst in the day. The thirty miles were covered in less than twenty-four hours, and Beves's infantry swung into Okanjande to find that the main water supply had been destroyed, and all that was available was a small well which gave nothing but the merest trickle. So another six miles had to be added to the day's march in order to reach the ample supplies of Otjiwarongo, but when the tired troops arrived there it was only to discover that the town supply was of the most meagre description, and that water was still another four miles off!

Onwards the brigade plodded , over the rocky track that cut through stout boots as though they had been made of paper, under a tropical sun and in blinding dust that obscured the whole landscape, until at last the promised water came in sight. Practically not a man had fallen out on the way— of such stern stuff were these South

Africans made—but at the end of the day in one battalion some five hundred strong nearly two hundred had to be treated by the medical officers for sore feet. Even so, but a very small proportion of these had to be left behind when the brigade resumed the weary trek to the north.

By this time it had become clear that if the enemy was to be brought to action at all, it must be by means of rapid movements on the part of the mounted troops. Accordingly, on June 27th, the 5th Mounted Brigade and Lukin's S.A.M.R. moved out of Otjiwarongo and pushed on to Omarassa, a march of thirty waterless miles. Five miles farther on is Okaputa, where there is good water, but from here to Otaviefontein is a distance of forty-five miles completely devoid of water. Having rested and watered the animals, the mounted men set out to cover the fifty miles to Otaviefontein, and completed the distance during the night of the 30th.

Early on the morning of July 1st Manie Botha's Free Staters reached the Elephant Berg, some five miles from Otaviefontein, and came into action against a strong force of the enemy who were well entrenched on the slopes of the Berg. The country hereabouts is exceedingly difficult, covered as it is by thick thorn scrub, in which it is next to impossible to locate the enemy until actually on top of him. The guns of the 2nd S.A.M.R. Battery were brought up, and opened an accurate fire on the enemy's trenches and *sangars*, which were soon rendered too hot for the liking of the Germans, who fled northwards without waiting for the assault of the dismounted troopers.

The pursuit was eagerly taken up by Manie Botha and his brigade, and so well was it driven home that the enemy was forced to continue his flight until he had reached the main German position in the Sarg Berg, south of Khorab Siding. In this affair we lost four killed and seven wounded, the German losses being about ten killed and wounded and twenty-five prisoners.

While this running fight was in progress, Lukin's brigade had borne more to the right to force the Eisenberg Nek, which was reported to have been heavily mined. The intelligence was not at fault, for the Nek, which affords the principal access to Otaviefontein, was found to be a veritable potential volcano. For nearly two hundred yards of its length it had been made the depository of cases upon cases of dynamite and almost literally of tons of scrap iron of every kind, from nuts to ploughshares. Fortunately, the luck that had attended the force in the matter of mines still held, and the main cable which connected the mines with the Hun observation post was quickly found and cut.

A party of S.A.M.R. was told off to follow the cable through the bush and find the post. They traced it up the slope of the Elephant Berg, and suddenly came upon the enemy explosion party, who were so busy in trying to make their exploder work—they were ignorant of the fact that the cable had been severed—that they did not notice the approach of our men, and were easily taken prisoners.

The occupation of Otaviefontein and the important railway junction of Otavi, meant that the Germans must now either fight or surrender. The only place in which they could make a stand was in the Sarg Berg, some ten miles north of the positions occupied by the Union force. But the latter had exhausted its supplies, and no forward move could be made until these could come up. Besides, the Sarg Berg position would probably—or, at any rate, possibly—have to be assaulted, and this could not be done until the infantry came up.

Beves arrived at Otaviefontein on July 4th, the brigade having marched forty-five miles in the last thirty-six hours. In all they had covered 245 miles in twelve days' marching. From the time they left Usakos they had never received more than half rations, and on the last six days of the trek they had lived on a biscuit and a half a day, with the addition of what meagre supplies of meat could be obtained from the countryside. No wonder that Beves, in a brigade order issued at Otaviefontein, expressed himself as being proud to command such troops! He had good reason indeed. Colonel Franke, the German commander, on being informed that the infantry had arrived, said: "Of course, they have been brought up by train." I do not think that to this day he believes they marched every foot of the way.

On the very day of their arrival an armistice had been concluded between the two headquarters, and arrangements were in progress for a meeting at which terms of surrender were to be discussed. This meeting took place on July 6th, as we shall see later. In the meantime a curious situation was developing out on the flanks. All touch had been lost with Myburgh, who, it will be remembered, had been entrusted with the enveloping movement on the right, and nothing had been heard from Brits, who was making north as fast as his horses could travel, far out on our left. A fragment of a wireless message from the latter had been picked up, but it only said that he had arrived at some unnamed place, so the news was rather worse than complete silence, since it conveyed nothing but that he was moving.

For hours the wireless threw its messages into the ether in the endeavour to regain communication with these commanders, but quite ineffectually. As things turned out, each of these dashing guerilla generals had accomplished a separate and dramatic *coup de main* which undoubtedly exercised no small influence on the result of the campaign.

On the day after the conclusion of the armistice news came in that Myburgh had actually occupied the town of Tsumeb, twenty, miles north of the German main position, capturing the whole garrison and a great store of arms, munitions and equipment. It has already been recorded that Myburgh set out from Okasisse and Wilhelmstahl on June 18th, and by the 26th his brigades had reached the foot of the great Waterberg plateau, capturing *en route* the military post of Okasongomingo and taking a handful of prisoners. The advance was continued across the plateau, where very difficult conditions were found to exist. Three days later Myburgh was at Otajewita, where the wells had been destroyed and the only available water was from a tiny spring which trickled from the mountain side.

There was nothing to be done but to press on another fifteen miles to Omboamgombe, where good water was supposed to exist. The brigades arrived there on the following day only to find the supply exhausted, and the troops were compelled to march still another ten miles to Esere. By this time the animals had been without water for two days, and were suffering severely from the strain of the rapid advance. To add to the hardships, the cold at night was intense, and it is recorded by Reuter's correspondent, who accompanied the column, that milk obtained at a farm by the wayside was doled out in frozen lumps in the morning.

Myburgh received intelligence on the morning of July 1st that a force of the enemy, estimated at about 800 with guns, was strongly entrenched in a *poort* near Guchab. Colonel Jordan, with the right wing of the 3rd Brigade and the Heavy Artillery, was sent by way of Asis to work round the enemy's left rear, the right wing of the 2nd Brigade being entrusted with a similar mission on the right. The rest of the force advanced at dawn of July 2nd, only to find that the Germans had evacuated the position during the night. Two days later Colonel Collins, with a wing of the 2nd Brigade, came into collision with a German force of about 500 men, commanded by Major von Kleish, and heavily defeated it, the enemy being hotly pursued and leaving about eighty prisoners in our hands. After this smart little affair the whole force moved on Tsumeb, with the intention of attacking the town next morning.

Colonel Jordan was in command of the troops detailed for the attack, and when his advanced parties were within four miles of Tsumeb itself they were met by a German officer, bearing a flag of truce, who had been sent out to inform General Myburgh that an armistice had been arranged and was in force. Myburgh at once dispatched Colonel Collins, under the white flag, to Tsumeb to endeavour to get into telephonic communication with General Headquarters at Otaviefontein. Before Colonel Collins returned, a staff officer arrived on the scene from General Botha with the explanation that the armistice was purely a local affair, with which none but the forces at Otaviefontein had any concern. Myburgh therefore sent in a demand for the immediate surrender of Tsumeb, failing compliance with which he threatened to attack at once. The German commander. Captain von Weiler, complied without further parley, and Myburgh's troopers forthwith took possession of the town. Huge stores of military equipment were found, sufficient for a force of ten thousand men, in addition to over five thousand cases of rum.

Myburgh had not been long in Tsumeb when news reached him over the telephone that Brits had accomplished a *coup* at once as daring and important as his own. This was no less than the occupation of the enemy's final base at Namutoni, fifty miles away to the north-west on the edge of the Etosha Pan. Not only had he occupied this important position, but he had captured the whole garrison, with ninety-two wagons, over two thousand animals, 550 cases of artillery ammunition, more than a million rounds of small-arm ammunition, and supplies sufficient to last the whole of the German forces for at least three months. In addition, forty-two British officers and over sixty other military and civilian British prisoners had been released.

It will not be without interest to trace the doings of Brits and his mounted brigades from the time they left Karibib, simultaneously with Myburgh's start from Okasisse. As we have seen, Brits occupied Omaruru on June 20th, and then went off to the north, into country that was almost entirely devoid of either grass or water. As an example of the conditions with which he had to contend, when the force arrived at Etanaho, after a thirty-mile trek, two wells were found, the water in which was so bitter that the parched animals refused to drink it, although they were suffering severely from thirst. The next water was twenty-five miles away at Omatjenne, so the brigades pushed on to that place, to be once again disappointed, the water supply having practically given out. Another forced march of ten miles had to be made to Otjitasu, where plentiful water was found. So maddened by thirst were the animals that several of the transport mules actually drank themselves to death! After a day's rest at Otjitasu Brits pushed off to Outjo, a German military post which was found to have been evacuated. A mountain gun, captured by the Germans in their attack on the Portuguese post at Nautila early, in the year, was taken here, but otherwise no spoil was left by the Germans in their retirement.

On July 3rd the column reached Ombika, sixty miles to the north of Outjo, and on the following day the police post at Okakuejo was occupied and a large quantity of dynamite taken and destroyed. On the 5th, Rietfontein, forty miles from Namutoni, was reached, and at the next water-hole, Springbokfontein, a German officer met the column, bearing a letter from the officer commanding at Namutoni, offering to surrender the place with the garrison and supplies. By this time the column had covered over 350 miles in thirteen marching days. Myburgh's record was something more than three hundred miles in fifteen days.

The position at this time, then, was that the German main force was concentrated in front of Botha at Otaviefontein, and was outnumbered by the forces at the immediate disposal of the latter. The German retreat was cut off from the north by Myburgh's mobile column, now at Tsumeb, and it was impossible for the enemy to break away to the north-west, his only effective line of retreat in any case. If he attempted to get away to the eastward he must be overtaken and destroyed by a combined operation of the forces disposed of by Botha and Myburgh. There were only two alternatives before Franke now. He must either fight it out to a finish in the position his troops now occupied, or he must take the line of least resistance and surrender on such terms as the Union commander-in-chief might feel inclined to offer. Even if he elected to take the more soldierly course and fight it out, there was very little hope for him, outnumbered and outmunitioned as he was.

It is a matter of history that he chose the discreeter part, but I am very much inclined to the belief that had it not been for Myburgh's dramatic capture of Tsumeb and the last reserves of the enemy's supplies, Franke would have fought at least one battle before throwing up the sponge. He could have adduced strong reasons for an attack. He knew as well as we did that the Union army had outrun all its supplies, and that delay was more dangerous to us than it was to him. He had at least a sporting chance of inflicting a severe blow on the invader if the luck had run his way at all, but it had not. The worst blow he could have received at the moment was the loss of his reserve supplies, and this he had sustained by the successful culmination of Myburgh's splendid operations.

CHAPTER 15

The End of the Campaign

It is now time to return to the things that were happening meanwhile at Otaviefontein. We know that an armistice had been arranged on July 4th for the purpose of discussing terms upon which hostilities could be terminated. There was much speculation as to the exact nature of the terms that General Botha would be inclined to offer. Seven weeks before, when our occupation of the colony was not nearly as effective as now, the only terms was unconditional surrender. Since then the Germans had been hunted from pillar to post, and driven out of every one of their important towns and posts. They were now without supplies, had no reserve ammunition, and were almost entirely surrounded in their last defensive position by an army vastly outnumbering their own. Therefore, it was argued, the terms they were likely to be accorded could scarcely be less onerous than they had been offered at Giftkop. However, as nothing was allowed to leak out in advance, we had, *faute de mieux,* patiently to await the issue of the conferences between the general and the German governor.

The first of these conferences took place at "Kilo 500" on the railway line on July 6th, at which the draft terms of surrender were handed to Governor Seitz, an answer being demanded by 2.30 a.m. on July 9th. The interval was occupied in getting up supplies and preparing to go on with the campaign in the event of the enemy's electing to reject the terms. Of course, all offensive movements of troops were suspended in accordance with the agreement under the armistice.

The night of the 8th was an anxious one for all. General Botha had made it clear that the answer was to be handed over not a minute after the stipulated time, and that if it were delayed he should take it that the terms were unacceptable and would act accordingly. The whole force was held in readiness to move out to selected positions immediately on the expiry of the allotted time, in anticipation that the enemy would, in the event of his rejection of the terms, try his fortune in a surprise attack. As a matter of fact, this is exactly what the Germans had prepared to do, and all their plans had been elaborated for an assault on the camp by way of the dry river bed. The attack was to be made with the bayonet, under the impression that they would only have to meet *burgher* troops, who were not equipped with the "white arm," and who, they anticipated, would be a comparatively easy prey.

The German is a good soldier. We must at least acknowledge that, whatever other qualities we are bound to deny him; but one of his manifest failings is that he does not seem to credit the opposition with knowing anything about the game. If he had elected to attack Otaviefontein that night he would have discovered that there were others who knew a little about the art of war. He would have found that instead of the dismounted *burghers*, armed only with rifle and handicapped by the darkness, he would have had to tackle Beves's infantry, who had been detailed to hold the river approach in anticipation of this precise form of attack. The Germans admitted that this had been their plan, and were vastly surprised when they were told that it had been foreseen and provided against. As a matter of strict fact, they did not know when the plan was laid that our infantry had arrived.

But the enemy was to accept the obvious. So, punctually at the time laid down, the German acceptance of the terms was handed over and another 350,000 square miles had been added to the British Empire. When the exact terms became known, it was agreed that they did not err on the side of harshness; they were certainly very far removed from the unconditional surrender of the Giftkop conference. The officers of the German force were to be allowed to retain their arms and the horses nominally allotted to them in their military establishment, and were to be allowed to live on parole at places selected by them.

The rank and file of the regular forces were to be interned in the colony, and each non-commissioned officer and man was to be allowed to retain his rifle, but no ammunition. The reservists, *landwehr and landsturm*, were to surrender their arms, and, after signing an undertaking not to take any further part in the war, were to be allowed to return to their homes and resume their civil occupations. This was to apply equally to those who surrendered under the terms and to those who had already been captured during the operations. The police of the colony were to be treated, so far as they had been mobilised, as active troops. Those members of the police who were on duty in distant parts of the colony were to be left at their posts until relieved by Union troops, in order that the lives and property of non- combatants might be protected.

Under the terms of surrender, civil servants of the Imperial German Government or of the Protectorate were allowed to return to their homes on parole, but they were, of course, precluded from in any way interfering in the affairs of the colony under the Union administration. The protocol of surrender was signed by General Botha, as commanding-in-chief the Union forces, and by both Dr. Seitz and Colonel Franke, representing the German civil and military administrations.

Immediately after the terms had been signed, the handing over of war material and the disarming of the surrendered troops was begun. In all, 4,700 troops laid down their arms, and the spoils of war included thirty-seven field guns and howitzers, with twenty-two machine-guns and a huge amount of ammunition and stores.

So ended a campaign that, though it scarcely produced a fight that could be dignified by the name of battle, especially in comparison with the colossal battles of Europe, was one of the most arduous of modem times in its demands on the determination and stamina of the armies engaged. The campaign was brought to a successful issue by a rare combination of consummate generalship and magnificent qualities of soldiership.

So far as we ourselves were concerned, we had orders before the surrender to return to Usakos, *en route* to other scenes and spheres of activity. The return over the roads that had taken us three weeks to cover on the way up, we negotiated without incident in as many days. At Usakos we were delayed for some days, awaiting instructions as to future movements, and then one day we said goodbye to the town we had come to regard with quite an affection—I have mentioned before that Usakos is a perfect little oasis in a desert land—and proceeded by road to Ebony, there to entrain for Walfish and embark for we knew not where. I think our entrainment at Ebony was a piece of work that is worth recording.

The whole of the cars, stores, motorcycles and the complete paraphernalia of the squadron were put into the trucks in two hours, and that from improvised ramps built of mealie bags! Not bad going at all, but everyone worked his best, for we had finished a successful campaign and were keen to get out of a country for which no one had any particular regard. And, we hoped, there was more work before us in another theatre.

Five more days we spent on the fly-ridden beach at Walfish before we embarked for Cape Town. It had been bad when we came out, but it was immeasurably worse now, when thousands of animals had been picketed in the meantime on its sandy shore. The whole place smelt like a huge stable, as in fact it had been, and as for the flies, they infested everything with their noisome presence. Food and drink were full of them, and it was impossible to get away from the torment of the things until the coolness of evening sent them to sleep. We tried everything we could think of to mitigate the nuisance, but they actually seemed to thrive on the remedies we evolved. Others of the hardships of South-West Africa we may forget, but the flies and the stench of Walfish will remain forever a memory of sordid misery. While awaiting transport, I received orders from home to detach one section for service in East Africa and return to England with the rest.

This was disappointing news all round. It meant the breaking up of the squadron in which we had all felt a real pride, and to whose future doings in some other sphere of the Great War we had looked forward with eagerness. However, orders were orders, and these were definite enough to admit of no qualification, so there was nothing to be done but to make the necessary arrangements in accordance with the behests of My Lords Commissioners. Nalder was detailed to go in command of the East African detachment with two officers and forty men, whose fortunes we shall follow later.

We at last received instructions to proceed to Cape Town *en route* for our several destinations, and finally arrived there without incident worthy of note. Once there, we were busy again with the overhaul of the cars intended for the East Coast and with the fitting out of the detachment, which was at last satisfactorily completed before the main body of the squadron departed for England. Before we left the Cape we had the satisfaction of receiving the thanks of the South African Government for our work in the late campaign. As this to some extent purports to be a rough story of the doings of the squadron before splitting up, it is perhaps permissible to quote the communication of the Governor-General of South Africa in which those thanks were conveyed. It took the shape of a telegram to the senior naval officer at Simon's Bay, and was as follows:

"Ministers would be glad if you would convey to the officer commanding the Naval Armoured Car Squadron their high appreciation of, and grateful thanks for, the valuable services rendered by that

Squadron in the German South-West African campaign. Ministers are informed by the General Officer Commanding in Chief the Union forces in the field that the conduct of the officers and other ratings of the squadron under all conditions and in all circumstances maintained the high traditions of the Royal Navy. Before squadron leaves South Africa Ministers would be glad if a suitable expression of their appreciation of its services could be conveyed to all ranks, together with the earnest good wishes of the Union Government for the Squadron's good luck and success in its future enterprises."

It is a matter of history now that, for reasons that are still obscure, it was decided, while we were actually on our way to England, to disband the whole of the R.N. Armoured Car Division. It is not, of course, permissible to discuss here the policy which dictated the action whereby a fine fighting force, with a magnificent record of service on all fronts of the war, was thrown to the dogs. When the whole history of the division, from its inception in the first days of the war to its breaking up, comes to be written, that policy, whatever the motives that prompted it, will be adjudged to have been totally wrong and mistaken.

So much has already been recognised in certain official circles. If confirmation of this view be needed, this is to be seen in the work of the surviving remnants which did not fall within the scheme of disbandment in consequence of their employment in remote theatres. The doings of these surviving detachments in East Africa under Nalder and Burningham-White, and in Russia under Locker-Lampson, are eloquent of the fighting stuff of which the Armoured Car Division was composed.

CHAPTER 16

The Earlier Operations

It was not until some months after the conclusion of the campaign in South-West Africa that I found myself once more in the Dark Continent, engaged in operations for the conquest of the last remaining German colony. In the meantime the Armoured Car Section detached from No. 1 Squadron for service in that theatre of war had been busily at work, and had rendered a very large amount of useful assistance in the operations directed towards keeping the Germans in check and preventing an effective invasion of British East Africa. The section arrived at Mombasa in the middle of August, and was at once pushed forward to Voi, a little more than a hundred miles up the Uganda railway, and attached to the force commanded by General Tighe, who was in charge of the whole campaign.

It will be interesting to review briefly the military position as it existed when Nalder's detachment arrived in the country. It will be within the recollection of the reader who has followed the progress of the Great War on all fronts and in all theatres that the first attempt to invade German East Africa met with disastrous failure. It had been planned to land an Indian brigade at Tanga, one of the two principal ports on the German East African littoral, and, after occupying the town and harbour, to use the place as a base for operations to be conducted up the Usambara Railway. The raid was well conceived, and the arrangements for its carrying out had been planned with all necessary elaboration. The execution, however, fell very far short of the ideal.

It would be out of place to indulge in detailed criticism of an operation of the kind, in which one has of necessity to judge by accounts at second-hand and by impressions gathered a year after the event. It must be recorded, however, that the Tanga episode, in its results and in its after-effects on the East African campaign, has to be set down as one of the most regrettable incidents of the war. It was not an enterprise on the grand scale, since it only involved the landing of a single infantry brigade. The casualties, though heavy in pro- portion to the number of troops engaged, were a mere bagatelle in comparison with those sustained in a single day's raiding activity on either of the main fronts, but in loss of prestige and its collateral raising of the enemy's low morale, it exercised a most pernicious effect on the local conditions.

Briefly, the story of Tanga is that a fleet of British transports, escorted by warships, suddenly appeared off the port. Instead of giving the Germans an hour to make up their minds to surrender or fight it out, they were given forty-eight hours, of which they took the fullest advantage. Troops were hastily rushed into the town, barbed wire defences were as hastily constructed, machine-guns mounted in the trees, and preparations were made to give the invaders a hot reception. At the expiration of the time set for consideration, the white flag was hoisted over the town. The brigade was landed and advanced to take possession. It was not until a part of the landing force had actually penetrated to the town itself that the Germans unmasked their preparations. The troops, who naturally imagined that all they had to do was to take peaceful possession of an undefended town, suddenly found themselves under a withering fire from rifles and machine-guns.

The native regiments broke and made for the beach, their flight being accelerated by swarms of bees from hives which the Germans had slung on wires among the trees and which had been stirred into madness by the simple expedient of firing a few bullets through the hives. The retirement was gallantly covered by the 2nd Loyal North Lancashires, who suffered very heavy casualties in so doing. The effect of the surprise, and the panic which had taken hold of the natives, was such that it was judged hopeless to make another attempt, and accordingly the whole force was embarked, leaving behind most of the dead, a number of wounded, and a substantial amount of material. When everything that could be saved had been shipped, the transports steamed off to sea, one of the escorting warships firing a few six-inch shells into the place by way of parting salute.

The material loss was comparatively heavy, but the moral effect was far worse. This was very well reflected in the tone of the German newspapers published in the colony before and after the Tanga affair. Before this the tone had been one of despondency. What was the use, they asked, of resisting an enemy who had the seas open to him and was thus able to throw overwhelming masses of troops into the country? The argument with which the Colonial German sought to lay unction to his soul—that the real issues would be decided in Europe—was brought out. There was no necessity, they urged, to risk the destruction of their towns and the ruin of their plantations, apart altogether from the loss of life that a prolonged campaign must entail.

The best thing to be done, then, was to make what terms they could, and submit with the best possible grace to a British occupation which would be very temporary, anyway. After the Tanga disaster the tone was entirely different. If this was the best show the British could stage, then there was not the slightest reason why they should do anything but fight things out to a finish. Not only could they hold their own colony, but there was the adjoining British East Africa that might even be conquered! Altogether the fiasco of Tanga was a most deplorable incident.

After this failure no further attempt was made at a landing on the coast of the German Colony. Indeed, the small British forces in British East Africa soon had enough to occupy all their energies without being committed to offensive enterprises from the sea. As this does not purport to be in any way a history of the campaign from its first inception, we may pass over the preliminary operations and confine our attention for the time being to the situation in the middle of August, 1915. Tanga I have only referred to because of its undoubted bearing on the subsequent events of the East African "side-show."

At the time of which we are speaking the Germans had succeeded in overrunning, and were in occupation of, a considerable area of British East Africa. In the west they had crossed the border near Longido, and at one time were seriously threatening Nairobi, the capital. Nearer the sea they were in occupation of Taveta, a small settlement ten miles inside the British border, and had entrenched camps at Mbuyuni and Serengeti, the first-named nearly thirty miles from the frontier. They appeared in force at Maktau, and their patrols even penetrated as far as Voi. From Voi to the sea they carried out systematic and frequent raids on the Uganda railway, and several times succeeded in blowing up trains conveying supplies to the force at Voi.

General Tighe had at his disposal a number of troops which was really inadequate to safeguard the border against the active enemy, let alone to carry offensive operations into German territory. For some months, therefore, he was compelled to stand strictly on the defensive. No troops could be spared from England, since at that time the new armies were still in the making. The whole of the energies of South Africa were absorbed in the campaign in South-West Africa, and there was manifestly nothing to be hoped for from that quarter until the successful issue of the operations on the other side of the Continent should set free the men who had been serving there under Botha. At times the situation approached the critical, as the pressure from the mobile German columns shifted its incidence from one point to another of the attenuated line held by Tighe's scanty forces. Fortunately, the enemy does not appear to have been too well served by his intelligence, and he seems to have been very much in the dark with regard to the exact number of men that the British commander had at his disposal.

In the early days of the campaign there is little doubt but that a strong enemy offensive must have produced the most important results. It is not at all improbable that Nairobi itself could have been taken, even if the Germans had been unable to hold it for long, but their operations were, on the whole, of a desultory, if most annoying, character. Indeed, the enemy command seems to have suffered from a similar sort of mental paralysis to that which so seriously hampered the German resistance in South-West Africa. In a minor degree it displayed intense activity which caused a great deal of annoyance, but it showed at the same time an almost inexplicable want of ability to realise the wider opportunities.

It may, of course, have been that Colonel von Lettow,[1] the German commander-in-chief, was, as I have said, badly served by his intelligence department, and supposed that he had much stronger forces opposed to him than was actually the case. This, however, is a hypothesis that hardly bears examination in the light of what we know of the perfection of the German espionage system all over the world. Later in the campaign we know that he was hopelessly at fault in his estimates of the numbers of British troops in the field, and believed that there were many more than were actually available, but in the opening stages he could have been under no such delusions, and one cannot but marvel that he did not attempt a really serious invasion of

1. *My Reminiscences of East Africa*: the East Africa Campaign of the First World War by the most notable German commander by Paul Emil von Lettow-Vorbeck also published by Leonaur.

the British Colony.

However, he preferred to carry on a series of relatively minor operations and allowed the golden opportunity to slip away. His opportunity persisted for sixteen months, until the conclusion of the campaign in South-West Africa released large numbers of South African troops for service on the other side of the Continent, Ultimately, of course, an invasion of British East Africa must have brought the Germans to defeat at the hands of the very much superior forces that were massed against them in the end. But defeat was certain in any case as soon as the British Government had leisure and men to spare for the work, and one would have thought that von Lettow would have taken the wider outlook and carried the war into the enemy's country. He was stronger in men, guns and machine-guns than the British at any time up to the end of 1915 and had ample military supplies, which had been accumulated over a term of years in readiness for "*Der Tag*," yet the most he was able to do with all his great advantages was to give the British a very uncomfortable and anxious time.

It is no part of my present task to seek for reasons or explanations of these failures of the enemy. They may have been due to some psychological peculiarity of the German colonial soldier, or they may have been less in the nature of failure to grasp the true military situation than consequent upon orders from Berlin. Knowing as we do the real military capacity of the German soldier and his ability to think largely, it would seem that the reasons are to be found in the latter alternative. It is quite possible that the Great General Staff had given its orders for the general conduct of these colonial campaigns, and had forbidden any dissipation of forces in offensive attempts, preferring to keep them intact for purposes of pure defence.

How else to account for the German passivity exhibited when chances of the offensive-defensive were simply begging to be taken, I cannot see. It was certainly fortunate for us in the case of East Africa that these things were as they were, for if we had had to clear a determined enemy out of the British colony, reinforced as he would have been by numberless recruits from the fighting tribes who would have been attracted to his cause by the prestige of conquest, the difficulties of the task would have been incalculably enhanced.

Sketch map of German East Africa

CHAPTER 17

Armoured Cars With Tighe

It has already been recorded that the armoured cars under Nalder were sent straight up to Voi immediately on their arrival in the colony. At this time General Tighe was endeavouring to push the construction of a branch line from Voi towards Maktau, thirty-eight miles to the south-west. The railway was to be a part of the general scheme of communications when the field force should have been brought up to a strength sufficient to enable it to clear the enemy out of the British territory then occupied by him, and to undertake in earnest the invasion and conquest of the last remaining German colony. Ultimately this line was to link up with the Usambara railway , which runs north- west from the German port of Tanga to New Moschi, and had been projected by the Germans as far as Aruscha. At the time of which I am speaking very little progress had been made with the extension, partly on account of the nature of the country and partly because of the enterprise of the enemy.

For the first few miles after leaving Voi the country is fairly open, and the only real difficulties encountered are on account of the heavy grades which cannot be avoided when laying a military line such as this. In the ordinary way, when time is not a vital essence of the contract, this becomes a comparatively simple matter of engineering, and the time spent on making cuttings to ease the grades is of no particular consequence. Here, however, was neither time nor labour available to engineer the road properly, and some of the grades are such as would grieve the heart of an English Board of Trade inspector.

After the first ten miles the line leaves the hilly country and enters the bush. There is nothing else in the world which is quite like the bush of tropical Africa, nor is there anything in language which can properly describe it to one whose ideas of dense vegetation are based upon an acquaintance with, let us say, the New Forest. Imagine, if you can, an almost impenetrable mass of thorn, ten feet high at the least and often much more—not a mere hundred acres or so, but many hundreds of square miles in extent. When you are well into it the bush deadens the strong tropical sunlight to soft twilight, and in it, unless you are a navigator or a trained bushman, you lose all sense of direction and locality before you have gone a hundred yards. You might as well be lost in the worst fog that even London can produce as take to the bush alone unless you know it, for you have as much chance of seeing or finding your way in the one as in the other.

And in a London fog you only risk the very temporary inconvenience of losing your way and being late for dinner. You may, if you have exceptionally bad luck, be run down by a motor-omnibus, but that is only a remote chance. But the bush carries other and even more exciting risks for the inexperienced or the unwary. There are the thorns for a start—not the thorns of the English hedgerows, but real thorns, wicked, hooked thorns, three inches long and a quarter of an inch thick at the base, that pierce the heaviest and strongest clothing and anchor you as fast as if you had been nailed to the tree.

When the real thorn of the "wait-a-bit" kind takes hold, you do not try force to disengage yourself, else you are only providing amusement for the thorn, and you will leave most of your clothing and no small proportion of your skin to decorate the tree. You simply go back and carefully unhook yourself lest worse befall. It is no use at all to be impatient—you are in the bush and must regulate yourself accordingly.

Even in peaceful times you are never quite sure of what you will meet in the bush. It may only be snakes, which no one minds very much. On the other hand, you may emerge into a clearing and find yourself faced by a leopard or even a lion, though, as a rule, the big cats like the bush itself as little as it deserves to be liked. You may come to water and blunder almost on top of rhino. Anything may happen at any time. But while the bush has no attraction in peace, it is the outside limit in war-time. There is only one thing of which you are sure when you plunge into it, and that is that you are going to be bitten by every kind of noxious insect that ever was since the Egyptian plague of flies. Beyond that, anything at all may happen to you. You probably know that the enemy is as intent upon stalking you as you are on getting him, so that every next bush and thorn tree may conceal the last surprise. You hate a clearing as the Evil One is supposed to hate holy water, because you know from bitter experience that in all probability your friend the Hun has planted a couple of machine-guns to sweep it. He knows that by the time you reach this particular clearing you will be utterly fed up with hacking your way through the dense vegetation, and that it will attract you as the candle attracts the moth. And, if you are foolish, or have not learnt his engaging little ways, the result will be pretty much the same in the end.

The worst of working in the bush is the impossibility of maintaining touch and communication. The meaning of the "fog of war" only becomes properly appreciated when you find yourself turned loose in the bush with a detachment of perhaps a hundred men. You set out full of confidence, and have got it all figured out that whatever may happen to others you, at least, are not going to lose either yourself or your detachment. Everything goes according to the plan until you have proceeded for perhaps a quarter of a mile, and then you begin to wonder what has happened and what has become of everybody. You can hear them, but as for seeing more than the half-dozen in your own immediate vicinity, that is entirely out of the question.

Presently you see a couple of men in your immediate front, partly obscured from view by the intervening growth. You know that none of your own people ought to be there, and you feel very much inclined to fire at them on the principle of its being better to be sure than sorry. Second thoughts prevail and you refrain, fortunately, for you discover later that they are stragglers from mother detachment who have lost their sense of direction and are trying to find their way back. Then you come upon a group of black soldiers who cause you some moments of acute discomfort, because you cannot make up your mind whether they are of that magnificent force, the King's African Rifles, or whether they are Hun *askaries*, whose uniform is almost identical save for a slight difference in the head-dress.

If your luck is in you are able to satisfy yourself that they are *askaries* before they detect your exact whereabouts, but it has to be very well in indeed if you, a mere white man, are going to catch the bush-bred native off his guard. It has been done, but not very often. In common with all who know him, I have a great respect and admiration for the native soldier; whether he be King's African Rifleman or German *askari*, he is as good a fighting man as you would ask to have beside you in a tight corner, or as worthy an enemy as the veriest fire-eater could desire as an opponent. He is first and last a soldier. He comes of stock whose business has been fighting for many generations, and he is thus rich in warlike tradition.

Full of courage, he is as faithful as a dog to his officers, if these know how to handle him and humour his prejudices. Watch him on the march and you will see him when he halts for even a short interval employing his leisure in cleaning his rifle until it is speckless without and within—no matter when or where, you will never find the native soldier with a dirty rifle. He has got it deep down in his childlike mind that his rifle is his only friend, to be cherished and tended against the time that it will be all that stands between him and sudden death. He cannot shoot, as a rule, and when you are opposed to him the safest place is usually in the firing-line. With infinite trouble you may make a third-class shot of him in about a year, but that is the best you can expect. But if he is not much of a shot he is a magnificent bayonet fighter, as might be expected when it is remembered that he is almost born with a spear in his hand.

Let him once get to close quarters with the "white arm" and he will give the best European troops as merry a scrimmage as they could want—and it will not be more than even money on the result. Sometimes, when he gets really angry, he will throw away his regulation weapons and betake himself to the use of the *panga,* the keen-edged cutlass that is given him to cut a way through the bush. Then is the time when nothing in the world will stop him short of death itself. Death he has no fear of—he has been brought up in its company, as it were, and wounds leave him with unruffled nerves. Like all native troops, he requires understanding and thinking for all the time, but once you have got his confidence he is yours to lead to the nethermost pit if needs be.

If it be necessary to send him to absolutely certain death it will never occur to him that he ought not to go—he will assume, if he troubles to think about it at all, that it is all in the game, and that the *Bwana* knows best, anyway. In the bush he is worth any two white men, because he knows it and knows its ways and the manners and customs of every living thing that is in it. Where the white soldier loses himself, the track is as plain to the native as the main Brighton road to a London motorist, and his way of finding his whereabouts in country he does not know is something approaching the uncanny. It is a thousand pities that, instead of three weak battalions of King's African Rifles we had not had a quarter of a million of the splendid black warriors of East and Central Africa under arms when the war broke out.

It was not too late even then to have recruited and trained large numbers of them for service in the tropical campaigns, but the time has gone by now when they could be usefully employed in this war. There has been much irresponsible talk of letting loose millions of black men to swamp the Germans by sheer weight of numbers. Well and good, if only it were possible, but it is not. We could probably get the men easily enough, but the problem is that of officers to train and lead them. It is not every regimental officer who can get on with the native, so that the field of selection is very much narrowed. Then there is the question of language. It takes time to learn even so simple a language as Swahili, and until the officer can meet his men on the common ground of mutual understanding it goes without saying that he cannot secure and retain their confidence. It takes two years to get a new formation into anything like working efficiency, and—well, the thing is obvious.

To return to Nalder and his detachment of armoured cars. Before their arrival the work of railway construction had been very much hampered by the enemy. Scarcely a day passed without the construction gangs having to suspend work on account of the threat of attack. The British patrols were constantly attacked, and the blowing up of the line by Germans from Mbuyuni, or from the post at Kasigau, was a weekly occurrence. These enemy parties displayed the utmost hardihood and activity in the prosecution of their operations, often coining close in to Voi itself.

A good road, fully capable of bearing the heaviest motor traffic, had been built beside the railway, with a view principally to its use by motor transport when the advance towards Kilimanjaro should be begun, and it was obvious that here the armoured cars could prove of the greatest value in patrolling the line and assisting in the protection of the construction gangs. They were at once given this duty, and it may be placed on record now that on no single occasion after the Germans first encountered them were our railway patrols attacked or was the line itself seriously damaged.

Nearly two months were spent by the detachment in the monotonous work of patrolling between Voi and Maktau, varied by an occasional plunge into the bush in company with mounted infantry patrols in the effort to round up the enemy's raiding parties. Long before this period came to an end the Germans had learnt to regard the cars and their crews with much respect. The native German troops, which as a rule are afraid of nothing, could hardly be got to face the

cars, which they called "the charging rhinoceros which spits lead."
After their first two or three encounters with these uncanny monsters,
as they regarded them, the natives seemed struck with a superstitious
terror, and several times when overtaken by the cars and called upon
to surrender they were simply too terrified to do anything but run
round and round in circles.

The Germans tried everything they knew to destroy or capture the
cars. They mined the roads, but the nearest they ever got to bagging
a car was one morning when Nalder himself had gone out with two
cars on a reconnoitring patrol. The leading car passed wide of a big
tree in a clearing, which marked the limit of one of our patrol areas.
It had been the custom for some days for the cars to proceed to this
point and remain under the tree for some time before returning—not
at all a wise practice in face of an active enemy who is studying your
habits with the same attention you are giving to his. Having observed
the procedure, the Germans set to work to prepare a surprise for the
next visit and laid a heavy mine under the tree, beneath the actual spot
on which the cars were wont to stand.

For some reason it had dawned upon Nalder that his cars might
possibly have been seen by the enemy, and he decided to give the tree
a wide berth on this morning. It was as well that he did so, for when
he had been in the neighbourhood for some little time a motor-lorry
came along with railway material. Fortunately, it was being driven at
a fairly fast pace, and, swinging towards the tree to clear the armoured
cars, it passed right over the mine, which exploded under the tail of
the lorry without doing anything worse than giving those on board
a severe fright.

On another occasion one of the cars was ambushed by a party
of Germans and *askaries* in the bush, who tried boarding tactics. The
venture was not at all a profitable one, since they were driven off with
the loss of several of the party killed and wounded, and five *askaries*
were brought into Maktau as prisoners. Closer acquaintance with the
"rhinoceros" had modified their terror of the beast, and, contrary to
their expectations, they had not been slaughtered out of hand, so they
arrived in camp full of hilarity and enormously pleased at the new
experience. There were not five more delighted niggers in all Africa
than these. They had enjoyed their first motor ride so much, in spite
of the untoward circumstances that had been responsible for it, that
they absolutely refused to get off the car and had to be removed by
main force.

Later, when the most advanced post held by the British became the entrenched camp at Maktau, the cars were employed mostly in reconnaissance work and patrols towards Mbuyuniy always in conjunction with the mounted infantry detachment of the Loyal North Lancashires under Atkinson and Story, and much good work was done between this period and the beginning of the forward movement early in 1916. There was not a day on which one or more of the cars was not employed in this way, and very few on which there was not some sort of a fight with enemy patrols.

It was in this kind of work that the armoured cars excelled, the combination between them and the "M.I." being just what was required for keeping the bush clear of the enemy's parties. The latter continuously displayed the greatest enterprise and daring. When Maktau was first occupied by the British a *boma* (thorn *zareba*) was built right round the perimeter of the camp, backed by trenches and machine-gun emplacements. Outside the *boma* the bush was dense, and there was nothing to prevent the enemy from coming right up to the camp without being seen. Night after night his parties worked up and fired through the *boma* into the tents. A favourite game was to creep quietly up and pitch a stone over the thorn abattis close to a sentry post. Until our people got used to it, it was ten to one that someone would start up to investigate the cause of the noise and would get shot for his pains.

As soon as we were firmly established at Maktau, operations were begun for clearing away the bush to the south, so as to secure a good field of fire, and it was during these bush-cutting operations that the combination did much of its good work. It was not to be supposed that so active an enemy as the Germans had shown themselves to be would allow our bush-cutting parties to work without interruption, and a most wearing system of protective patrols had to be carried out. The moment news of enemy parties was received out would go a couple of cars and a detachment of M.I. The business of the latter was carefully to shepherd the Germans out of the thick bush on to the road or into the comparatively clear country to the south-east, so that the cars could work under favourable conditions.

Several times a considerable measure of success attended these little affairs, and very materially increased the respect in which the enemy had already come to hold this very effective combination. So highly did the Germans esteem it in the end that they at last ceased altogether to worry the working parties. It was common report that their native soldiers refused to go anywhere where the ears were likely to be encountered. Flesh and blood they could understand, and were perfectly willing to tackle at any time and in the most desperate circumstances, but these silent monsters, which seemed to enjoy being shot at and which came on under the most murderous rifle and machine-gun fire, were beyond them.

By the end of 1915 the time of severe crisis had passed and fresh British and South African troops were beginning to arrive. General Sir H. L. Smith-Dorrien[1] had been appointed to take over the chief command, and was on his way out from England. There was talk of fresh divisions from home, besides at least two infantry brigades from South Africa and a further two or three mounted brigades under the well-tried leaders who had led them in the conquest of South-West Africa. There could be no offensive against the German forces which were in occupation of a large tract of British territory until the bulk of the reinforcements should have arrived, but the little force that had been hanging on so gallantly for months was able to feel that it had endured the worst, and that the time was now fast approaching when the tables would be turned and they would be the harriers instead of the harried.

1. *Smith-Dorrien: Isandlwhana to the Great War* by Horace Smith-Dorrien also published by Leonaur.

CHAPTER 18

Smuts Takes Command

It was in November of 1915, after the return of Lord Kitchener from his last journey to Eastern Europe, that it was decided that a real effort should be made to accomplish the conquest of German East Africa. It has already been seen that the forces at the disposal of General Tighe were barely adequate to the task of holding the border between the British and German colonies, and that unless he were heavily reinforced he would be hard put to it to hold his own, while the idea of his being able to embark upon offensive operations was altogether out of the question. Accordingly, preparations for a campaign on a large scale were at once initiated.

General Smith-Dorrien was appointed to command, and with Brigadier-General Simpson-Baikie as chief of the staff, began to organise so much of the detail as could be arranged in England. He left home on December 23rd for the Cape with most of his Staff. In the meantime I had been offered an appointment for "special service" with armoured cars by General Simpson-Baikie, and, although this entailed leaving the naval service and being transferred to the army, the prospect of active service in the tropics was too tempting and I accepted.

It is a matter of history now that General Smith-Dorrien was unable to take the field on account of severe illness. I have heard opinions expressed to the effect that his illness had something of the diplomatic about it, and that there were other reasons why he did not proceed farther than the Cape and gave place to General Smuts. It may be as well to place it on record that nothing could be farther from the truth than this rumour. How it originated I do not pretend to know, nor does it matter now. This I am able to say of my own knowledge, that by the time Madeira was reached on the passage out, General Smith-

Dorrien was so ill that he would have been landed there if it had been safe to move him. He could not be landed and had to be taken on to the Cape, and so ill was he that no one expected he would live to reach Cape Town. However, he did live, as we know, but it was obvious that he would not be able to stand the severe strain of a prolonged campaign in a tropical country, and he did the only thing possible by resigning his command.

Unfortunately, the general's illness was responsible for some amount of delay in completing the final arrangements for the campaign, and it was not until February 12th, just over a month after General Smith-Dorrien's arrival at the Cape, that General Smuts was appointed to be commander-in-chief in East Africa, and sailed from Delagoa Bay for Mombasa to take over the direction of the campaign. Two days later General Smith-Dorrien and General Simpson-Baikie left Cape Town on their return to England. The hiatus in the command had not, however, interfered with the reinforcing of the East African contingent. The Second South African Brigade (Infantry) under Beves and a part of the Third Brigade under Berrangé left South Africa in January and arrived in Mombasa during the first days of February, enabling General Tighe to push on with his preparations for the long-delayed offensive. It will now be useful to glance at the features of the military situation as it existed when General Smuts assumed the chief command.

The force at the disposal of the German commander at this time was estimated to consist of about 2,000 whites and 14,000 native troops, with sixty guns, including several 4.1-inch naval guns which had been landed from the wreck of the *Königsberg* after her destruction by the monitors *Severn* and *Mersey* in the Rufiji River, and about eighty machine-guns. These troops were organised in companies, averaging about 200 strong, with 10 *per cent*, of whites as officers and non-commissioned officers, and with two machine-guns per company. The extent of British territory in enemy occupation was, roughly, the same as in August of the previous year, and the only appreciable difference in the situation was that the German offensive activities had been somewhat checked as a result of the British reinforcements which, by the beginning of the New Year, had already arrived in the field.

In addition to the frontier town of Taveta and the advanced posts at Serengeti and Mbuyuni, the enemy had a strong garrison on the Umba River, from which he could threaten the Uganda Railway, while the post at Kasigau was still in his occupation. A complete reorganisation of the British forces was now carried out and two divisions were formed, with the necessary lines of communication troops.

By the middle of January the 1st Division, under Major-General Stewart, was concentrated south of Kajiado and the Magadi Soda Lake with a view to the occupation of Longido, west of Kilimanjaro and just within the Ger- man border. This operation was carried to a successful issue with only slight opposition, and the enemy retired southwards towards Geraragua and Moschi. A few days later the 2nd Division, under Brigadier-General Malleson, advanced from Maktau and occupied the entrenched camp at Serengeti after a smart little action. It was in this action that McMullen, the medical officer attached to Nalder's detachment of armoured cars, performed the act that gained him the Distinguished Service Cross.

It was reported to him that an officer was lying wounded in the long elephant grass south of the camp. One of the cars had already made an ineffectual attempt to find him, so McMullen went out with two men of the detachment, all on motorcycles, and scoured the grass under very heavy machine-gun fire until at last they discovered the wounded man and brought him in. In addition to the D.S.C. gained by the doctor, the two petty officers who accompanied him were awarded the D.S.M. From all the accounts I heard from eyewitnesses it was a most gallant deed, and the honours accorded to the plucky trio were thoroughly well deserved.

With the arrival of Beves's 2nd Brigade early in February, General Tighe felt himself strong enough to assume the offensive, and accordingly determined to make a reconnaissance in force of Salaita Hill and, if possible, occupy the German position there. This decision of Tighe's brought about an action which has probably caused more discussion, not unmixed with a little ill-feeling, than any other operation of the campaign. Salaita was an exceedingly strong position. Imagine a solitary steep hill, planted in almost impenetrable bush, with the natural difficulties of the position increased tenfold by skilful preparations for defence carried out by an enemy who knew his business down to the last details and had had unlimited time to make them.

If Salaita had stood in the midst of a bare, open plain, it would still have been a hard nut to crack, but as it happens to be surrounded by every conceivable natural difficulty the task of capturing it by infantry attack, unless with an overwhelming superiority in numbers, was one to tax to the utmost the most soldierly and most highly disciplined troops.

General Malleson was entrusted with the arrangements for the attack, and had at his disposal six battalions of infantry, drawn from the 2nd South African and 1st East African Brigades, supported by eighteen guns. After a lengthy artillery bombardment of the enemy's trenches on the hill, the infantry were sent forward to the assault. It was the South Africans who came in for the brunt of the affair. After working their way through the dense bush almost to the foot of the hill, they discovered that the real German defences were not on the hill itself, but well in advance of its lower slopes. The bush had been cleverly wired, and every little clearing was commanded by machine-guns concealed in the trees. Some desperate fighting took place before these outlying annoyances could be disposed of, and presently the three battalions found themselves faced by the enemy's main position, consisting of a series of trenches disposed in a masterly way.

Colonel Freeth's battalion was the first to taste of the reception prepared for them. They were advancing against a line of trenches which they took to be those of the main position, when they were suddenly assailed by heavy blasts of machine-gun fire from the right flank. Under the impression that this was the real position which had thus suddenly been unmasked, Colonel Freeth rapidly changed front to the right, with the intention of attacking the new front, but before the movement had been completed the battalion came under heavy fire from what was now its rear. The brigade was in a trap, and a very deadly trap too. Only by a rapid retirement out of the zone of fire, for the purpose of reforming the battered ranks, could the situation be saved. The retirement was begun, and surely no movement of the kind was ever conducted in more unfavourable circumstances.

It was not the strength of the enemy in front of the brigade, or that the casualties sustained by the latter had been heavy enough seriously to impair the moral of the men, that made the task of the South Africans so difficult. The bush was so thick that it was utterly impossible to preserve any semblance of formation, and the men broke up into scattered groups, sometimes with an officer or non-commissioned officer to impose the hand of authority, but more often entirely without any measure of control. To increase the confusion, the moment it was realised by the enemy that the surprise he had prepared for the South Africans had in truth come off as he had planned, he counter-attacked with the greatest gallantry. His native troops emerged from the trenches at the double, and rushed forward with the bayonet to complete the rout which the German command believed had been accomplished.

But he had reckoned without his host, for, although the moral of the South Africans had been shaken, it was by no means broken. Besides, the reserve battalion of Beves's brigade had not fallen victims to the surprise, and, with the 130th Baluchis, was at hand to deal with the enemy's irruption. At once the counter-attack was checked, and the enemy, finding that he was, after all, not to have everything his own way, withdrew to his trenches again.

It was during this phase of the fight that Sub-Lieutenant Marshall performed an act of the greatest gallantry, which was quite characteristic of him, as he had proved himself in the previous campaign. Marshall, in command of two of the Naval armoured cars, had worked close up to the first line of the German trenches when the surprise fire was sprung upon Colonel Freeth's battalion. In an instant he realised what the inevitable result must be if the enemy was allowed to counter-attack while the battalion was in process of changing its front to conform to the new situation.

Without the least hesitation he pushed forward with his cars and had the good fortune to come upon a gap between two trenches, which enabled him actually to get in rear of the German first line and to get both his maxims into action at close range. The effect of this exceedingly bold and skilful act was that the enemy in the immediate vicinity of Marshall's two cars was pinned to his trenches and suffered a great many casualties into the bargain. The cars remained in position until the gun which Marshall himself was working had its water-jacket pierced by a bullet and was put out of action. This decided him to withdraw, for the double reason that he was now almost helpless for defence or offence, and, moreover, his presence of mind and pluck had produced the intended effect, so that there was now no sense in remaining where he was. He had found his way in by accident, but the trouble now was to find a road out through the thick bush.

Up and down in front of the German trenches ran the cars, searching for the gap through which they had entered. The one gun was out of action and ammunition for the other was running perilously short. It began to look as though there was nothing for it but to disable the cars and make the best of a thoroughly bad situation, when just as things appeared most hopeless, the way out was discovered by two motorcyclists who were working with the cars. With a parting burst of fire from his remaining gun Marshall made a rapid exit from a position that had long ago ceased to be comfortable.

Marshall was personally thanked by Beves for his gallantry and

skilful initiative which undoubtedly had the effect of seriously interfering with the German counter-attack, at any rate, at the point at
which he so opportunely brought his guns into action. I was exceedingly pleased to know of Marshall's conduct on this occasion, since I
had marked him during the campaign in South-West Africa as a particularly capable and gallant young officer who, given the opportunity,
was sure to distinguish himself beyond the ordinary.

One of the main purposes of the reconnaissance had been achieved,
and the enemy had been compelled to disclose his real position.
The hill had been reconnoitred repeatedly by the aeroplanes of the
R.N.A.S., which were working with the land forces, and a number
of excellent photographs had been taken of the defences on the hill
itself. But it was obvious that much that these photographs disclosed
was in the nature of dummy preparation, designed to deceive our
aerial observers, and it became certain that the real position was else-
where than on the hill. So well had the enemy prepared his real position that no known method of reconnaissance could have disclosed
it, concealed as his trenches were by the thick, tangled screen of bush
that runs right to the foot of the hill and beyond. From the air, even at
low altitudes, they were completely invisible, and to approach on foot
without blundering right on to them was impossible.

After the retirement of Beves's men, General Malleson decided
that enough had been done for the day and that he would withdraw to Serengeti with his whole force. This movement was successfully carried out without any molestation by the enemy. Naturally, the
South Africans felt sore at the result of their first experience in this,
their initial essay in bush fighting. Many of them were fresh from the
victorious campaign in South-West Africa, where they had learned to
regard the German capacity for resistance with something very like
contempt.

Furthermore, they knew that the bulk of the enemy's troops in
front of them were natives, and to your true South African a native is
a "nigger" and to be appraised accordingly. We have never recruited
and disciplined the South African tribes, else the men of Salaita would
have known that the despised "nigger" is as good a fighting man as
needs be when he is properly trained and led by European officers
in whom he has learned to feel confidence. But they did not know,
and they thus went into action with a feeling of "cocksureness" that
received a very nasty jar indeed.

Let me hasten to say that I am not at all writing in any spirit of criticism of men who afterwards proved themselves to the full to be gallant soldiers, comparable to the best the Overseas Dominions have sent to the help of the Motherland in her hour of agony. I place the facts on record firstly because they *are* facts, and secondly because the record may assist the reader to an understanding of the real calibre of the opposition that our gallant troops have had to encounter in the conquest of East Africa. Moreover, it may serve to point a moral to others who may be inclined to discount the fighting value of the native soldier. Smuts himself sums up Salaita very well in his first dispatch dealing with the East African operations when he says, rather grimly:

"The South African Infantry had learned some invaluable lessons in bush-fighting, and also had opportunities to estimate the fighting qualities of their enemy."

They had indeed. How much they had learned and how well they availed themselves of their lesson will appear later, when the story falls to be told of the desperate gallantry with which these same troops carried the Latema-Reata ridge by a midnight bayonet charge in the face of an appalling fire. The Salaita affair took place on February 12th, the day that Smuts sailed from South Africa to take over the command. It was a week later, on the 19th, that he arrived at Mombasa, where he was met by General Tighe, and assumed the active direction of operations.

The first question he had to decide was whether it was feasible to initiate an offensive which would clear the high, fertile country of the Kilimanjaro region before the setting in of the rainy season. As a rule, the "big rains" may be looked for late in March, and generally continue throughout April until the middle of May. Then comes the dry season, which extends until October, when the "little rains" are to be expected. These rainy seasons are really a rather variable quantity, as regards the date of their beginning and their duration. They have been known to fail altogether, as, for example, in 1914, when there were no "little rains" in the coast belt.

On the other hand, in 1915, both big and little rains were abnormally heavy. During the rainy seasons movements of troops on anything approaching a large scale are quite impossible. Roads disappear and become channels down which pour raging torrents. The country sloping down from the heights of Kilimanjaro and Meru is very much akin to the "black cotton" soils of India, and, under the influence of the pelting tropical torrent miscalled rain, becomes a spongy slough into which men sink up to their middles and pack animals to the girths. Guns and transport vehicles are immovable, so that even if troops could be moved they could neither be fed nor supplied with ammunition or stores.

What Smuts had really to decide was whether he would gamble with Nature. If the rains were a little late—even if they held off until the average normal date, he would have time to complete the conquest of the most fertile and most desirable portions of the German colony before his operations were brought to a halt by the coming of the rainy season. A more timid commander would have preferred to have been certain, and no blame could have attached to him for his decision. There were good reasons for the adoption of the more cautious policy. Although Smuts had at his disposal by this time a force that he considered amply strong for his initial purpose, there were reinforcements on the seas that would have rendered success assured. Many of the last arrived units were new formations, unacclimatised to the country and quite unused to working in the bush, while of the troops who had been working longest most of them had been decimated by fever and diseases peculiar to the country and were badly in need of rest.

On the other hand, the enemy still occupied a considerable extent of British territory, and his prestige with the native tribes stood high and was increasing every day. It was known that he believed our forces to be far stronger than they actually were. As a matter of fact, we knew afterwards that he estimated them at more than twice the number we ever had in the country. Therefore, if the great forward movement could be made before the German commander had had time to ascertain the real truth, his self-deception would be worth a great deal to us. After weighing all the *pros* and *cons* of the situation Smuts decided for the bolder course, and at once set to work on the modifications of existing dispositions rendered necessary by his decision. What those dispositions were, and how well the new commander's anticipations worked out in the result, we shall see in the next chapter.

CHAPTER 19

Preparing the Offensive

General Tighe's plan for the general offensive had been first to occupy the Kilimanjaro area through a converging movement, simultaneously carried out from Longido and Mbuyuni as soon as he should have sufficient troops at his disposal to enable him to initiate such a combined operation with a reasonable prospect of success. Kahe, on the Usambara railway, was to be the objective of this advance. Smuts decided to adhere to the plan, but considered that some modification of dispositions was necessary in order to avoid frontal attacks against entrenched positions in the dense bush, and to ensure the rapidity of movement that was essential if the operations were to be brought to a successful issue before the coming of the rains, which could hardly be placed later than the end of March. Accordingly, van Deventer's mounted brigade, then at Longido with Stewart, was transferred to Mbuyuni to act directly under the commander-in-chief in a turning movement to the north of Salaita and Taveta, and by the beginning of March all the minor concentrations made necessary by the changes in detail of the

plans initiated by General Tighe had been completed. Apart from the redistribution of forces already in the country, the bulk of the 3rd South African brigade, under Brigadier-General Berrangé, had arrived and was at Smuts's disposal.

At this date the distribution of the troops was as follows: The 1st Division, commanded by Major-General Stewart, was at Longido, awaiting orders to begin its advance towards Moschi by way of the Engare Nanjuki River and through the gap between Kilimanjaro and Meru to Boma Ngombe. The allotted task of Stewart's division was to sweep aside the resistance of the enemy in front of him, and then press on to Kahe with the object of cutting the German communications by the Usambara railway. The division had in front of it a waterless belt of desert, some thirty-five miles wide, and the country farther on was expected to prove very difficult for transport; besides which, it was quite on the cards that Stewart would find the enemy's opposition strong enough seriously to delay his advance. Moreover, he had farther to go than the columns that were to start from Mbuyuni, so he was to be given a start of two clear days before a move was made from the more easterly point.

The column which was to operate from Mbuyuni was to consist of the 2nd Division under General Tighe and van Deventer's 1st South African Mounted Brigade, and was to advance through the gap between Kilimanjaro and the Pare Hills. It was to undertake an offensive against the main German force, which Intelligence reports indicated had been concentrated near Taveta, with strong detachments at Salaita, at Lake Jipe, and in the bush to the eastward of the Lumi River. It was estimated that the total force concentrated by the enemy in the Kilimanjaro area was approximately six thousand strong, with sixteen guns and thirty-seven machine-guns. The 1st Division was to move on March 5th from Longido.

At nightfall on the 7th the 3rd South African Infantry Brigade and the 1st Mounted Brigade, both under the command of van Deventer, were to leave Mbuyuni and Serengeti and make a night march to the Lumi, east of Lake Chala. If all went well, these troops ought to be in position on the morning of the 8th, in order to seize the high ground round Lake Chala and develop a turning movement against Taveta. The object of this turning movement was, as General Smuts says in his dispatch describing these operations, partly to take the enemy by surprise and partly to avoid the necessity for frontal attacks through the thick bush which lay between Salaita and Taveta.

This was not perhaps altogether "by the book." It meant leaving a strong enemy detachment sitting across our communications at Salaita and giving the main German force an opportunity of breaking back past the left flank. Smuts's plan evidently was to turn the Salaita position and drive the enemy to the east into the Pare hills, and then by the use of the mounted troops to envelop his forces in such a way that he would be obliged to fight a battle that would, if all went according to plan, be decisive. Unfortunately, matters did not progress "according to plan," and, as a matter of strict historical accuracy. Smuts did not at any time succeed in compelling the Germans to fight a decisive action. By means of rapidly carried-out enveloping movements the

Germans were evicted from all the best and most fertile areas of the Colony, but the fact remains that they were always able to elude the final decisive stroke that would have destroyed their army. Their better knowledge of the country in which they were operating, and the fact that they were not hampered by many of the considerations which limit the rate of advance of an invading army, gave them just that margin of superior mobility that enabled them to avoid being brought to serious action, and left them at the end of the "campaign of eviction" with their forces practically intact.

As the campaign progressed instances multiplied in which, by all the laws of probability, the German forces were almost bound to have been destroyed utterly, but the foe was able to slip through before the net had been too tightly drawn for escape. The strategic conception of Smuts's campaign was sound enough, and he was gallantly backed by every one of his subordinate commanders, but fate and the character of the country were against a quickly decisive result. But to return to the story of the operations of the March campaign.

The 2nd Division was ordered to advance against Salaita on the morning of March 8th and to entrench a line facing the hill, while the Force Reserve was to follow van Deventer during the night of the 7th and take up a position astride of the Lumi River, in readiness to reinforce either van Deventer or the 2nd Division, as might be found necessary. Smuts himself accompanied the Force Reserve, with his personal staff, in order to keep closely in touch with the operations around Taveta. All the initial movements were carried out with complete success. The 1st Division succeeded in safely crossing the waterless belt, and established its advanced posts at Engare Nanjuki late on the afternoon of the 6th. On the following day Stewart's whole division was concentrated at this point, and was moved on to Geraragua on the 8th. All was now ready for the opening of the preliminary operations.

Early on the morning of the 8th van Deventer reached the Lumi, near the southern end of the Ziwani swamp, and the 3rd Infantry Brigade almost simultaneously arrived on the river, a little to the east of Lake Chala. General van Deventer at once made good the high ground lying between Chala and the Rhombo Mission station, and proceeded to make a converging movement on the German position at Chala from the east and north-west, at the same time threatening the enemy's line of retreat to the south. The German detachment at Chala quickly decided that these operations had made the position untenable and withdrew towards Taveta. Van Deventer's people pursued the retiring enemy right into Taveta itself and actually occupied a portion of the town, but as the Germans were in considerable force a retirement on the Chala position was decided upon.

While these operations were being carried out by the mounted men the 3rd S.A. Infantry Brigade and the Force Reserve had been halted astride the Lumi to guard the crossing. The outposts of this force were attacked several times during the afternoon by an enemy detachment of about 500, which the sudden move on Chala had caused to be separated from the German main body. All these attacks, which were made through thick bush, were repulsed with comparative ease and some considerable loss to the enemy.

Simultaneously with the operations around Chala and Taveta, the 2nd Division had entrenched in front of the Salaita position while a heavy artillery bombardment—which did little actual harm—of the defences of the hill was carried out. It had been the intention to push home an infantry attack on the morning of the 9th in the event of the enemy's deciding to hold on to Salaita, or the more probable contingency of the garrison's finding itself cut off by the rapidity of our movements towards the Lumi. When, on the afternoon of the 10th, the infantry went forward to attack the hill, it was found that as a result of the bombardment, in conjunction with the turning movement towards Chala, the Germans had evacuated the position during the night. Two squadrons of the 4th South African Horse had been sent to intercept the enemy's retreat, but the latter got clear away without serious interference from the mounted men.

Taveta was made good on the 10th by a regiment of the South African Horse from Chala. The town was occupied without resistance, but only just in time to forestall a strong enemy force which had been sent back with the obvious intention of occupying it. This force was engaged and compelled to retire in the direction of Latema-Reata, but it fought a stiff rearguard action with the pursuing South Africans, and was finally left in occupation of the Latema ridge, which was soon to be the scene of one of the stiffest fights of the campaign. It was obvious that the enemy had been seriously disturbed by the sudden completeness of Smuts's offensiveness and must have been entirely deceived as to the number of men at the latter's disposal. Had he not been uncertain of the real significance of the movements he must have made a stand at Taveta, which had been thoroughly prepared for defence. Instead, he allowed himself to be rattled out of the place long before there was any necessity for him to go, while the state of uncertainty in which he found himself is still further evidenced by his attempt to reoccupy the position after it was too late. Taveta was an important capture for us, in that it stands astride the only road to Moschi, the terminus of the Usambara railway. Moreover, it had the additional moral value of being—from the local point of view—the one considerable British town held by the Germans at this time.

It was outside Taveta, on the day of its occupation, that I renewed acquaintance with the naval armoured cars which had served with me in the campaign in German South-West, and heard from Nalder the story of their doings since we had parted at Cape Town six months before. The last time I had seen these cars in the field was in the illimitable desert of South-West, with never a green thing to break the arid red-grey of the granite landscape. Here they were waiting on the edge of a vast mangrove swamp until the bridge over the Lumi could be repaired sufficiently for them to cross.

In front was a clearing perhaps a hundred yards wide, but otherwise tropical bush prevented one from seeing more than a dozen yards in any direction. The last time I had seen them at work the want of water was the most pronounced disability. Now the excess of it was the main trouble, for the country in the valley of the Lumi is either of the "black cotton" variety or else a powdery red soil which is almost equally spongy and moisture-retaining, and thus very difficult for heavy cars to work in.

Naturally, everything being on the hurry up, as it were, we had very little time to spare for the interchange of experiences, particularly as we were expecting to be attacked at any moment by the German detachment which, as I have already recorded, had become separated from the main body and was wandering about the bush at a loose end. If they had only known it they had the chance of their lives that afternoon. Guns, transport, cars of every size, power and purpose, had come pouring down the road from Mbuyuni hot-foot for Taveta, and the check at the Lumi was something to be remembered.

For a mile back from the river the road was choked with every sort of vehicle. There was no room in the bush for the fighting troops to work on any coherent sort of plan, and a sudden attack on the convoys would have played ducks and drakes with the whole column. Either the enemy did not realise his opportunity or his heart misgave him, for he simply confined himself to the few sharp attacks on the outposts already spoken of, and avoided what would have been a real opportunity. But then the story of war is really one of lost and unrealised opportunities which, had they not been so lost or left unrealised, would have profoundly modified the course of the history of nations.

By this time it was known that the Germans had withdrawn from Taveta in two directions. Part of their forces had retired by the Taveta-Moschi road towards the west, while another portion had gone by way of Latema and Reata by the Taveta-Kahe road. The line of retreat of their main body was still uncertain. Our mounted troops were in touch with a force, which appeared to be merely a rearguard, between Taveta and Moschi, while a body of unknown strength was in position on the *nek* of the Latema-Reata ridge. It was thus essential to clear up the situation in order to determine whether this was merely a covering force or whether the Germans were in sufficient strength here to threaten a counter-attack towards Taveta. In any case, it was impossible to advance beyond Taveta while the *nek* was still in possession of the enemy.

Smuts accordingly decided to attack the *nek* and, if possible, make good the position. The troops immediately available for the enterprise were three weak infantry battalions, two field and one howitzer batteries, a mounted infantry company, the machine-gun section of the 2nd Loyal North Lancashires, and the East African volunteer machine-gun section. The three infantry battalions were the 130th Baluchis, the 2nd Rhodesian Regiment, and the 3rd King's African Rifles. General Malleson was given command of the operations, and, after a preliminary reconnaissance of the ground, selected as his objective a spur dominating the *nek* from the north. The approach to the spur was over very difficult ground, the bush being very thick over the slopes running up to the ridge, and it was evident that the task before the assaulting troops was going to prove one of no small difficulty, particularly in view of the weakness of the three battalions on which the brunt of the attack was to fall.

However, the troops of the Force Reserve were due to arrive in Taveta almost at any moment, and would be available to reinforce the attack if the enemy proved to be in real strength. Moreover, it was absolutely essential that the situation should be cleared up without delay in view of the serious results that were likely to accrue from a counter-attack in force while our own troops were moving into position. It was decided in view of all the contingencies that the attack should be carried out at once, without waiting for the expected reinforcements actually to arrive on the scene.

CHAPTER 20

The Battle of Latema-Reata

It was a little before noon on the 11th that Malleson's brigade began its advance on the ridge, with the Baluchis and the K.A.R. in the firing-line, the Rhodesians forming the general reserve. The advance of the infantry was supported by the guns, which came into action at a range of a little under four thousand yards, while the mounted infantry were given the task of watching the flanks. Not until the first lines of the advancing infantry began to lose themselves to sight in the bush covering the slopes of the rise did the enemy disclose himself. When at last he decided that the time had come to make his presence and intentions known the rifle and machine-gun fire that burst forth all along the flanks of the slope was positively appalling. But the attack was in the hands of troops who had learned what fire really is. The Baluchis had not served in the trenches of Flanders to be daunted by mere noise.

The King's Africans had been in the field since the beginning of the campaign and, besides, came of fighting stock which does not know the meaning of nerves where anything short of the supernatural is concerned. The Rhodesians, too, were a veteran battalion which had been long in the field, and had been recruited among the very best of the British Colonial elements. Such troops as Malleson was leading to the attack of Latema were not to be deterred by trifles. But the bush was so dense and the enemy's fire so heavy and accurate, that even they could make very little head against the determined defence.

It is instinctive, when working through thick bush, to make for a clearing. It assists one in getting one's bearings, and, besides (as I have already been careful to explain), the very sight of a clear space fascinates by its promise of a cessation from the arduous toil—for it is all that—of forcing a way through the tangled, thorny undergrowth. The

Germans knew the fatal fascination of clearings, and had every one of them carefully covered by machine-guns, so that the moment any of our people emerged into the open they came under a devastating fire that accounted for a large proportion of the casualties sustained in the early stages of the fight. In addition to the machine-gunfire, which proved so deadly, the enemy had the advantage of the possession of several pom-poms, which he used with considerable moral, if little material effect.

I know of nothing more demoralising in this sort of fighting than the fire of this particularly devilish gun, which searches every foot of the ground over which you have to advance with its streams of little shells that seem to arrive as though they had been squirted from a hose. It is true they are not value for money when that is measured by the tale of casualties they cause, but there is nothing more calculated to make the men of the opposition keep their heads down than really well-directed pom-pom fire. And whatever failings as a soldier the German may have, and even he is not perfect despite all his schooling in the military art, if there is one thing he has little to learn about, it is the use of the machine-gun, whether it be pom-pom or rifle-calibre weapon.

Invariably he has a sure and certain eye for the best machine-gun position. He knows exactly when to open fire so as to produce the maximum of effect for a given expenditure of ammunition, and he never makes the mistake which so many young machine-gun officers are prone to fall into of hanging on too long. In a word, he is a past-master in the tactics of the machine-gun, and applies his knowledge altogether admirably. Wherever we met him, it was always his machine-gun fire that stood out as the one thing that was properly controlled and effective. The rifle fire of his *askaries* was always beneath contempt—half a mile behind the firing line you might become a casualty from the enemy's rifle fire.

Closer up you might be hit, because accidents are .always liable to happen even when African natives are behind the rifles, but if you were hit you could be very certain that it was not intentionally. But the machine-gun fire was another matter altogether, and if a man exposed himself anywhere within range of a German gun he was exceedingly lucky to escape with a whole skin.

Towards evening the troops of the Force Reserve began to arrive, and the attacking battalions were reinforced by the 5th South African Infantry. About this time General Malleson, who had been seriously indisposed all day, requested to be relieved, and the command of the attack was assumed by General Tighe. The latter at once pushed forward the Rhodesians, with orders to assault the Latema ridge in co-operation with the King's Africans and the Baluchis. Two more field batteries had by this time come into the fight in support of the assault, which was pressed home with the greatest gallantry, but completely failed to achieve its objective. It was in this phase of the action that the K.A.R. lost their commander, Lieutenant-Colonel Graham, who was killed while gallantly leading his men. General Tighe threw in half the 5th South Africans in support of the attack, but still no headway could be made in face of the heavy fire and the difficulties of the bush.

At about eight o'clock in the evening the 7th South Africans arrived from Taveta, and were sent by Smuts to reinforce Tighe's brigade. Their arrival decided Tighe that the only way the attack could succeed was by sending the two South African battalions in with the bayonet during the night. The decision was a daring one and one that carried more than a little risk with it. It is by no means disparaging to these two fine battalions to say that they had had very little training in bayonet fighting, while the native troops they were being asked to attack with the white arm were adepts at the game. The ground over which they were to advance was unknown, since there had been no opportunity of reconnoitring it, nor was it known even approximately what number of men the enemy had available.

True, the volume of fire developed did not argue that he had many rifles in his front line, but then it was his machine-guns that had held up the advance all day, and there was no pressing necessity for him to disclose his full strength. Against this was to be set the fact that the bush along the line of the *nek* did not appear to be very thick, and the moon was in its first quarter, which meant that there would be plenty of light for developing the attack up till midnight. But even if there had been stronger reasons against such a night attack than there were, the South Africans would have been keen to try it. They had been smarting under the lesson of Salaita for weeks, and they wanted a chance to wipe out the memory of its bitterness.

Lieutenant-Colonel Byron, of the 5th, was in command of the night advance. His own battalion formed the first line, with the 7th, under Freeth, in support. The plan of attack was for the 5th to go straight for the *nek* itself, while the 7th, on reaching the crest, were to wheel outwards by half-battalions and occupy the heights to the north and south of the *nek*. The attack was carried out with the greatest *élan* and daring, but the bush proved to be much thicker than it appeared, and there was a good deal of inevitable confusion during the rush up to the crest in the face of strong opposition by a stubborn enemy.

Men found themselves without officers, and officers lost touch with most of their commands, so that before long a steady trickle of men began to come down the slope. It was not a disorderly retirement by any means. On the contrary, there was far less confusion than might have been reasonably expected in the adverse circumstances of a night attack through thick thorn bush. The men mostly did exactly the right thing. They came quietly back and re-formed on the 1st East African Brigade, in readiness to go in again when cohesion should have been restored.

In the meantime Freeth and his second-in-command, Major Thompson, were gallantly carrying out the task assigned to them of occupying the high ground flanking the *nek*. The former made his way up the steep sides of the ridge of Latema. By the time he arrived at the crest he had only eighteen men with him, but nevertheless he proceeded to make good his position, and was presently joined by a few Rhodesians and King's African Rifles who had clung to the crest since the abortive assault of the afternoon, and the gallant little party hung on where they were until daylight. Thompson, on the Reata side, had had better luck, and managed to dig himself in with about 170 men in a position dominating the *nek*. Both he and Freeth received the well-deserved award of the D.S.O. for their services on this night.

The attack on the *nek* itself had not progressed much better than the flanking adventures. Colonel Byron met with the most stubborn resistance, and gained the crest of the *nek* at midnight with about twenty men. Finding that the enemy still dominated the ground gained, and that it was impossible for him to advance farther, or even to remain where he was, he withdrew his small force and retired down the hill. An hour later Tighe sent the 130th Baluchis forward, but they only got up in time to find that Byron had been compelled to retire and that Freeth and Thompson could not be communicated with. In all the circumstances, it was obvious that it was of no avail to attempt to retrieve the failure.

The moon had gone down, the night was as black as pitch, and with all the good will in the world—and there was enough of that to go round—it was clear that if the job could not be done by moonlight, it was hopeless to contemplate, that is to say, to attempt its renewal in the dark. Tighe therefore ordered the men to dig in astride the road and wait for daylight.

The subsequent happenings are interesting for the light they throw on the military genius of Smuts. It was a case of Salaita over again— the enemy was in possession of a strong position, against which we had in vain rammed our heads in a frontal attack. Very well; let them keep it in the meanwhile, and when the time was ripe they would find it quite untenable by reason of the things that were in process of happening somewhere else.

After receiving General Tighe's report. Smuts decided that it was inadvisable to press the frontal attack, and that it would be best to await the result of a turning movement by the mounted troops, which movement had already been ordered. Accordingly, Tighe was directed to withdraw from the line on which he had dug himself in. While his retirement was still in progress, patrols sent to endeavour to get into touch with the flanking detachments on the Latema and Reata ridges came in with the news that the enemy was in full retreat, and that the parties under Freeth and Thompson were even then in full occupation of the position.

No doubt the determined nature of the attacks, and particularly the night charge of the South Africans, had badly shaken the moral of the enemy's troops, but the ultimate cause of his abandonment of a position which he had demonstrated his ability to hold against frontal attack was undoubtedly the threat of envelopment and the cutting of his retreat to the Usambara railway at Kahe. The enemy left behind in his retirement a field gun, three of his precious machine-guns, and a quantity of ammunition. What casualties he sustained in the fighting it is scarcely possible to estimate. In all, about seventy of his dead were found after the engagement, but his losses were probably very much heavier than these figures would denote, since he was generally very careful to remove his dead and wounded. Our own casualties amounted to nearly three hundred killed and wounded—not a very extravagant number in view of the character of the fighting and the importance of the results achieved.

While these events were happening to the east of Taveta, van Deventer was feeling his way cautiously along the road running west to Moschi. He met with but slight opposition, though the enemy destroyed all the road bridges as he retired, and Moschi, the railway terminus, was successfully occupied on the 13th. It was unfortunate that difficulties of transport had prevented Stewart and the 1st Division from keeping to the time-table designed by Smuts. Had he been able to adhere to it, and been astride the road to Kahe when van Deventer was before Moschi, a blow might easily have been inflicted on the enemy which would have had the effect of shortening the campaign very materially. It was not until the 14th that Stewart and van Deventer joined hands at Moschi, by which time the enemy force of some six companies, which had retired by this westerly road, had made good its retreat to the Ruwu and Kahe.

For the next few days there were no troop movements of any importance. Not only was it necessary to consolidate the gains, but it was essential to improve the road between Taveta and Moschi, along which all the supplies for the force operating to the westward would have to pass. The road was in a general condition that could only be described as poisonous, if I may use this expressive and picturesque term. I have seen worse roads—most of the country we worked over in South-West was worse—but not very much. For five miles on either side of Taveta it was simply appalling and quite unfit to carry a heavy volume of motor traffic, which it would have to do if it was to be of any use. With the rainy season approaching, it was hopeless to depend upon animal transport, because the whole of the district is country where the dreaded tsetse fly abounds, and neither horses nor cattle can exist for any length of time.

I am by no means an authority on "fly" and have little acquaintance with its habits, but of its deadliness to animal life I do know something. Horses and cattle bitten by the tsetse will often work on quite happily for two or three weeks—until the first rain comes, and then their dissolution is rapid. Later in the campaign, when the rains had set in, van Deventer's mounted division lost half its horses in a little over a month, principally as a result of the fly and horse sickness. It will be readily recognised, then, that the first essential to any further advance was to get the roads into a decent state of repair.

By dint of the most strenuous labour the worst parts of the Taveta road were made good by the 18th, and reconnaissances were carried out towards the Ruwu River and the Kahe position. From now until the 21st there was a good deal of desultory fighting, some of it of a severe character, as when the enemy attacked General Sheppard's 1st Division at Store on the night of the 20th. (Sheppard was now in command of the division, in place of Stewart, who had returned to India.)

The objective of the operations which had now developed was

135

the capture of the line of the Ruwu, and particularly of the strong position at Kahe. Of course, Smuts's favourite manoeuvre of a wide turning movement again came into evidence, and it was curious to see how absolutely the story of the fight at Latema- Reata repeated itself in these later operations. Van Deventer was dispatched from Moschi with the 1st S.A. Mounted Brigade, the 4th South African Horse, and two field batteries, with orders to cross the Pangani River and get in rear of the position at Kahe station. He experienced considerable difficulty in carrying out his instructions, not only on account of the nature of the almost impenetrable bush, but through the constant opposition of the enemy. However, he succeeded in his task, and occupied in succession Kahe and Baumann Hills and Kahe station.

As soon as van Deventer's movement had developed, the troops under Sheppard were ordered to advance and attack the enemy position, which was on the edge of a clearing in the dense bush, with its flanks resting on the Defu and Soko Nassai Rivers. Sheppard's intention was to have used the 3rd S.A. Infantry Brigade to envelop the enemy's right flank, at the same time delivering a frontal attack with the remainder of his force. The advance of the 3rd Brigade, however, was so much impeded by the density of the bush that it failed to come into action in time to produce any decisive effect.

Sheppard's infantry made desperate attempts to cross the clearing in front of the German position, but the enemy machine-gun fire was too heavy and well-directed, and each attempt was beaten back with loss. No progress had been made when night fell, and the troops were ordered to dig themselves in, with a view to renewing the attack on the morrow, when the 3rd Brigade would be able to make its weight felt.

At dawn next morning, however, our patrols found the German position empty, and the enemy fled in the direction of Lembeni under the threat of van Deventer's envelopment. He had left behind him an interesting souvenir in the shape of another of the 4.1-inch guns landed from the *Königsberg*. This gun, which was in a fixed position, and another similar gun on a railway truck, had been in action against van Deventer during the whole of the 21st, and had been blown up by the Germans before they abandoned it. These were the heaviest guns the Germans had against us. I asked one of van Deventer's officers afterwards what he thought about these naval guns. He remarked, rather naively, "Well, they didn't do any harm, but the noise was rather terrifying."

While these operations were in progress, Aruscha had been occupied by mounted scouts, and the conquest of the richest part of the German colony was completed in very little more than a fortnight's strenuous campaigning. Thus by the genius of a great soldier had the position been completely reversed. At the beginning of March the enemy was not only holding on to all that was his before the war, but he was in occupation, as we have seen, of a very considerable area of British territory. By the end of the third week of the same month he had not only been ousted entirely from the British area, but had lost the most desirable part of his own dominion, with its vast plantations of coffee and other produce, and its wonderful potentialities of development.

More than his material loss, he had suffered the humiliation of severe defeat in the field and a consequent deterioration in the moral of the native troops who formed the bulk of his forces. The weakness of the native is that he does not understand the meaning of the tactical retreat. He is quite able to grasp the necessity of retreating when he has been soundly beaten in a square fight, and he will come again after he has been beaten, but he knows nothing of the niceties of the retirement to elude a turning or enveloping movement which is taking place somewhere beyond his ken. He is very likely to ascribe it to something else than the soldierly appreciation of an impossible position, and to lose heart and confidence in the leader who seems to him an adept in the art of running away to avoid coming to grips with his enemy.

Another by no means insignificant morale effect was likely to be produced on the native mind by the conquest of the Kilimanjaro area. I believe that the natives have a legend that whoever possesses the beautiful mountain—Kilimanjaro is surely the most beautiful of solitary peaks—will rule the whole country. The value of such an impression on the superstitious African mind is too obvious to be discounted.

The result of these preliminary operations had been all that the most exacting of commanders-in-chief could have wished. Indeed, so rapid had been their success that it had almost outrun organisation, and a halt had to be called to reorganise the forces for the next forward move, and to rest the troops after the arduous work of the month. A chain of outposts was accordingly established along the Ruwu, General Headquarters was removed to Moschi, and all the troops who could be spared were sent to the healthier localities to recuperate, while the work of preparing transport and supply went forward.

Two batteries of armoured cars were almost due to arrive from England, and I was sent down to Mombasa to superintend their disembarkation and to bring them up to the front as soon as they should be landed and fit for service. This meant a few quiet days in Mombasa, but I cannot say that it is a place I should recommend as a pleasure resort. Of course, being practically on the Equator, one expects it to be hot. Personally, I like the tropics, but Mombasa is too much like an oven to appeal to anything but a salamander. There is only one cool spot in the place, and that is the veranda of the club in the evening, when the sea breeze has gained some strength, but even then you cannot help remembering that a little later you will lie under a mosquito net and perspire as though in a seven times heated Turkish bath.

But any kind of civilisation is preferable to active service in the bush—or, at any rate, I would rather put it that even Mombasa affords a welcome relief to the everlasting tracklessness of interior Africa, with its perennial dirt and never-ceasing plague of insect pests. I don't know why Europeans choose to live in such places, unless, perhaps, it is for the purpose of extending hospitality to poor soldiers. They certainly do that, as I know from pleasant experience.

CHAPTER 21

Preparing the Second Campaign

The batteries which I had been sent down to receive arrived from England towards the end of March and were rapidly disembarked at Kilindini. Without delay they were moved by rail to Voi, and thence proceeded by road to Mbuyuni, where, it was understood, we were to spend the rainy season. A good deal was to be done before we could hope to go forward. There was not a single spare part or replacement for any of the cars; not a tyre nor a spare wheel for either armoured cars or transport vehicles had been brought out with them, nor was it possible to discover that any were on the way. This opened up a very pleasing prospect indeed, for unless spares arrived from home before the next forward move began it was difficult to see how the cars were to participate.

It is all very well to run risks when they are unavoidable, but to take heavy armoured cars into the African bush with no means of making good defects or of repairing the inevitable minor casualties entailed by the rough work these cars had before them, seemed to me to be going farther than was justifiable. The only armoured ears of the type in the country were those that had been working under Nalder, and although I had sent round with him the whole of the spares and replacements we had taken to South-West, I knew I could not rely on him for help, because of the rapid rate at which he had been compelled to use them. As a matter of fact, he himself was almost stranded for want of certain essential parts for his own cars.

I reported this matter of shortage to G.H.Q., and was instructed to go to Nairobi and see what I could raise in the way of car stores there. Nairobi was as badly off—I could have anything except what was required! However, urgent cables were sent to England requesting the immediate dispatch of the necessary stores, and with that much done I had to return empty-handed to Mbuyuni. By this time G.H.Q. had been established comfortably at Old Moschi, and thither I betook myself to report the result of my visit to Nairobi. My instructions were to strip the one battery of wheels and all parts that I considered essential in order to keep the other in the field for two months, and to report when the work had been accomplished.

That, of course, meant that the one battery was to be completely demobilised to put the other on its feet. My reflections were somewhat bitter when I thought of the fine organisation of the naval armoured car force, with its simply priceless personnel, which had all been blown to the four winds when, for some obscure reasons, it had been disbanded six months before and then revived in this piecemeal fashion under another organisation, hurriedly got together and as hurriedly sent on active service entirely without essential equipment. However, there was this much of comfort in the situation, that whatever the shortcomings in this one direction, we were at least well supplied with the actual fighting material, and if we could manage to equip and keep one battery going it would be something to the good.

It will perhaps be interesting, as well as serving to preserve continuity, to glance briefly at the situation at this time in its relation to the future of the operations about to be initiated. It has already been recorded that the mounted troops under van Deventer had occupied Aruscha late in March. This place constituted a convenient *point d'appui* for an invasion of the interior, directed against the central railway from Dar-es-Salaam on the coast to Ujiji on Lake Tanganyika. For some reason the enemy failed to appreciate the possibilities of an advance along this line, and withdrew the six companies which had originally been before Stewart in his advance from Longido and attached them to his main force in the Pare hills. This left only a weak detachment to oppose van Deventer farther west, and it was this fact that determined Smuts to make an advance in force and to aim at Kilimatinde, on the Central Railway, without waiting until the cessation of the rains which were now due at any time.

Another factor that weighed in the decision was that the rains are most violent in the Kilimanjaro-Aruscha district, while farther to the west and south they are usually much lighter, and are not of a character to hold up military operations entirely. The main difficulty was to concentrate the necessary force at Aruscha and initiate the forward movement before the rains broke and made movement on the roads converging on Aruscha impossible. The whole of the 2nd Division was to be employed in these operations, while the 1st and 3rd Divisions were to remain in quarters until the end of the rainy season made possible a resumption of the campaign against the enemy's main force nearer the coast.

This bold stroke was expected to result in the Germans being compelled to detach a considerable force from the main body to deal with van Deventer, in which case Smuts could reinforce the latter and still retain under his own hand sufficient troops successfully to carry out an offensive against the depleted enemy in the Pare and Usambara hills. It was a big conception and one that required considerable moral courage to pursue. There was the risk that the rainy season might prove to be of more than average severity, in which case van Deventer might find himself isolated in the interior, without the possibility of getting supplies of food and ammunition and with resultant risk of disaster.

As a matter of fact, something very nearly resembling this did happen eventually, when the Germans realised the potent threat of van Deventer's rapid movement on the nerve centre of the colony. Most of their supplies and recruits for their native army were drawn from the Tabora district, which was threatened by Smuts's far-seeing strategy, and they were compelled to take measures to stave it off, measures that came almost within reach of success, but for the soldierly skill of van Deventer and the constancy of his South Africans.

On April 1st the headquarters of the 2nd Division were at Aruscha, with the 1st Mounted Brigade and two batteries, while the infantry of the 3rd Brigade was on its way. In the meantime van Deventer had not been idle, and had pushed his detachments forward as far as Lolkissale, about thirty-five miles to the south, where they had come into contact with a strong enemy force defending the only water supply in the vicinity. On the night of the 3rd the mounted brigade was moved quietly out of Aruscha, and by daylight had completely surrounded the German force, which was in position on a rocky hill.

The ensuing action lasted throughout all the two following days, when the enemy surrendered with nearly five hundred men, of whom seventeen were whites, and two machine-guns. Some stores and a number of pack animals also fell into the hands of van Deventer's people, but not the least important capture was that of documents, from which it was clear that Colonel von Lettow intended to reinforce the posts at Ufiome and Kondoa Irangi, which were the first objectives of

141

the British advance. In the light of this information. Smuts ordered the advance to be pressed with all possible speed by the mounted troops, while the infantry was to follow up as rapidly as circumstances would permit.

This brings us to the time at which my own people were exerting all their energies in the task of getting the one battery ready for immediate service, in order to take part in this forward operation under van Deventer. What we could not strip off the cars of the other we had to improvise. For instance, originally every car had been equipped with a shield for the maxim, but these had all disappeared after the cars had been taken over from the navy. So to take their place we procured steel railway sleepers, cut them into three, and by cutting a gun-port in each end and fitting a clamping arrangement to grip the water-jacket, we got two excellent bullet-proof shields out of each sleeper. At the end of a week I was able to report that the battery was fit to take the field, and received orders to take it on and report to General Berrangé at Aruscha.

I knew that it was going to be a touch-and- go business with the rains. If we could negotiate the eighty odd miles from Mbuyuni to Aruscha in three or four days, we should be all right. If not, then it might be weeks before we could get up. Already there were reports of heavy rains to the north of Meru, and a mechanical transport column of light cars had taken the best part of a fortnight to cover the distance, and only got through by dint of the most strenuous exertions on the part of officers and men, with the assistance of gangs of natives. However, the people who knew the country averred that these were not the "big rains," but only the forerunning showers.

So, on April 7th, we set out from Mbuyuni on the first stage of the journey and arrived at Taveta without incident, save that a good deal of delay was caused by the badness of the roads in the Lumi valley. The next day's march was to New Moschi, and this was also easy. Roads were quite good, and had been improved by the pioneers, so that they were not much inferior to a third-class country road in England. On the 9th we left Moschi with the intention of getting right through to Aruscha if at all possible, but as events turned out we were not to make the acquaintance of that place for another five weeks.

For the first half-dozen miles the road was not bad, and it was only when we reached the crossing of the Kikafu River that we began to encounter real difficulties. The rains of the previous week had swollen the current so that it ran like a millrace and the water in the ford was more than axle deep, while the approaches were slippery and rough, with a gradient of about one in five for half a mile on either side of the ford. By lashing pieces of tarpaulin over the radiators and wrapping cloths round carburettors and magnetos to keep out the water, we eventually got the cars across in about three hours, though two of the armoured vehicles stopped in the middle of the ford through water in the magnetos, and had to be hauled out by manpower.

Even when the cars were across our difficulties were by no means at an end. None of the engines was pulling well, and to get four tons of car and armour up a steep, slippery slope, with a surface like an exaggerated sheet of corrugated iron was sheer man-killing work. However, it was managed at last, and we reached Somali Houses the same night. We had only covered a bare quarter of the distance assigned for the day's march, but still I thought we had not done at all badly. At Somali Houses we found the 9th South African Infantry, under an old friend of the South-West campaign. Colonel Kirkpatrick, and Bottomley's 12th South Africans, both these battalions being, like ourselves, en route to join van Deventer.

Very heavy rain fell during the night, and in the morning the roads were far too bad for the cars to move, though the rain had ceased and a hot sun promised well for later in the day. The rain held off, so that we were able to move at noon, and reached the Sanja River that night. The crossing was bad, but nothing like as difficult as that of the Kikafu, and we were able to get everything across with very little delay. The infantry moved on the same night, in order to cross the waterless belt which extends from here to Rasthauser during the cool, dark hours. We deferred our departure until daylight next morning, since it is quite impossible to move heavy cars—or any cars, for that matter—on these roads in the dark.

In some respects this day's march was one of the most strenuous we had to make, and was reminiscent of some of the hardest of our days in South-West Africa. The country is rocky, and huge boulders outcrop from the road, making advance by low-hung cars like our armoured vehicles a matter of considerable difficulty. In half a dozen places it required two or three hours' work with pick and shovel by all hands to make progress practicable. The worst places were in a series of steep *dongas*, where the best we could do was to ease off the edges of the rock, so as to make the road a little less like a great staircase, and then to let the cars bump down with all the brakes hard on and screaming.

At one place in particular I know everyone else thought it was impossible to get the cars down without smashing them. But I had seen what could be done with armoured cars on the other side of the Continent, and this place was not as bad as some I had seen safely negotiated, so we tried it and got them all down safely. All the same, I was very much relieved when the last car was at the bottom. It is one thing doing these perilous feats of driving with people who know their cars, but quite another when they have no experience of this kind of motoring acrobatics.

After we had safely crossed the rough, waterless belt, the road on was not bad as far as the Ussa River, but here we again met difficulties. There were two arms of the river to be crossed. The water in both was fortunately low, but the gradients leading down to the fords were steep and the track was very severely cut up. All the cars had to be assisted up the farther slopes by the united manpower of the battery. What this means under a powerful tropic sun and in the damp, enervating heat of the East African bush cannot be described—it must be experienced to be appreciated. By the time everything was across and at the top of the grade, all hands were in the last stage of physical exhaustion, so I decided to camp here for the night and make an early start in the morning.

During the night, however, the rain came down as it can rain only in the tropics, and by morning the road had been transformed into a veritable morass for a mile on beyond our camp. However, the rain had ceased and I was anxious to make Aruscha before the breaking of the real rains, so I decided to risk a move. I might have the cars hogged, but we might just as well be stuck in trying as to stay still and watch the roads grow worse.

We had now got into the river country, which was intersected by numerous small streams, the crossing of which meant in every case man-handling the cars up steep, greasy slopes and entailed the grimmest kind of hard labour on everyone, officers and men. But all were keen to get on, and in spite of the abject discomfort of tropical deluges by night and never-ceasing labour by day nobody grumbled, but put his back into the work in the determination that whoever else was to be out of the picture the armoured cars at least would be up in time. In the end we were to find that the forces of Nature were too strong for us, but it is to be put to the credit of the non-commissioned officers and men of the battery that they most loyally responded to the calls made by their officers on their endurance and fortitude during a time of extreme hardship.

We had been very seriously hampered by the lorry carrying our reserve ammunition, which was not powerful enough to negotiate the heavy grades, and which was so top-heavy as to be dangerous on the slippery mud of the hill-side roads. In many places these roads—tracks would be a better definition—had a slope downwards of forty-five degrees, and on many occasions we found it necessary to take the cars along singly, with as many men as could get near holding the car up to prevent it from slipping sideways down the *kloofs*. Several times our ammunition lorry had taken complete charge and skidded itself into positions which entailed hours of work to get it back on the road. After a good deal of consideration I determined to abandon it and push on with the armoured cars alone. It was taking risks, because we were on a road bare of all other troops and open to attack by the enemy, but then it was obvious that if I did not drop the lorry we should never get through at all. So it was left with a small guard at the crossing of the Tengeru, and we pushed on in the endeavour to reach Aruscha with at least the fighting portion of the battery.

A mile on from where we had left the lorry was a very bad river crossing—the worst we had yet encountered. Not only were the approach gradients long and steep, but the ford was deep and full of heavy boulders, so that before we could attempt the crossing we had to spend a couple of hours in removing the bigger stones to make the ford practicable for the cars. On the farther side the road sloped away heavily towards a low cliff, with a twenty-foot drop into the bush below, and in ascending this one of the armoured cars was driven over the edge through the glare of the setting sun in his eyes preventing the driver from seeing the road.

Fortunately, the car did not go bodily down the slope, but it lay in a very bad position for getting it back on the road, and we had no gear for carrying out salvage operations of this kind. There was nothing for it but to leave it until daylight and then do the best we could to salve it, so I decided to get the rest of the cars up the hill and camp there. To enhance our difficulties, the rain came down all night with torrential violence, and the whole countryside took on the aspect of a vast lake. However, it fortunately ceased to rain towards daylight, and as soon as the sun was up I made a start to get the stranded car back on to the road. We had to cut down trees to shore up the rotten earth of the cliff side and build a platform under the wheels before it was safe to attempt to move it, but after about four hours' work we had the satisfaction of once more seeing the car safely on the road again.

Nevertheless, our troubles were now thick upon us, because the road had become so bad owing to the rain during the night that it was quite impossible even to attempt to get the salved car to the top of the hill. The rain held off during the morning, and by the middle of the afternoon it became practicable to move things again, so after a couple of hours of heavy work in cutting branches to make good the worst places, we got the car up the hill by dint of much man-handling. Although all hands had had a strenuous day, I determined to move on and, if possible, reach the Kidjenge swamp that night, but about a mile farther on the road resolved itself into a veritable slough of despond, into which the cars sank above their axles.

There was no hope of moving them, and not a dry spot within miles to form a decent camping-ground, and to make matters worse the real rains broke this night. Fortunately, there were a few native huts close to where the cars were bogged, and in these the men were able to huddle as best they could. As a rule, such native dwellings are to be avoided like the plague, for they are hot-beds of every tropical disease known to medical science, but in this case I decided that the possible risk tick-fever, or something of the sort, was preferable to the malaria and dysentery that would follow the exposure of exhausted and unac-climatised men to the torrential rains in this unhealthy part of Africa.

During this night I had an experience at which I have often laughed since, but at the time I did not consider it any laughing matter. I had made myself as comfortable as circumstances would permit in my own car, and was trying to get to sleep when suddenly I heard the sound of heavy gun-fire, apparently three or four miles away. It grew in intensity until it assumed the volume of a bombardment, so I called a sentry and asked what he made of it and why he had not reported it. He agreed that it was gun-fire, but thought it was unnecessary to report it, as it was so heavy he was sure I must have heard it!

As the firing did not grow less, in about half an hour I walked along to the hut where the officers were sleeping and warned them to keep handy, as it seemed certain that the Germans were attacking Aruscha in considerable force. It was of no use to turn the men out— they were utterly exhausted with the strain of the day's work—and, in any case, the firing was too far off immediately to concern us, while, if we had been seriously attacked later, I did not want to have to meet it with men who, in addition to being physically exhausted, had had the heart washed out of them by standing to arms in the bitter rain and darkness. After about two hours of incessant firing the cannonade died away, and, having given instructions to the N.C.O. of the guard that I was to be called immediately if anything exceptional happened or was heard, I went back to the car and settled myself down to sleep again. By this time it was about two o'clock.

Hardly had I made myself comfortable when I was brought back to life by the sharp sound of machine-gun fire immediately in front, and apparently not more than a few hundred yards away. Then, while I was making up my mind about it, there was another burst of about ten rounds' rapid fire, and the sentry came up and reported a machine-gun in action. There was something in the sound, however, that I was not quite satisfied about, so I asked the sentry if he were certain that what he had heard was, in fact, a machine-gun. He was most positive that it was, and while he was in the act of asserting his belief there came another and then another burst of rapid fire.

I have never heard a German gun fire groups of from five to fifteen rounds, as this one seemed to be doing, and yet I knew that we had no one on the road in front, so that if it was a machine-gun it must be an enemy one. Still, I was not satisfied, and sent for the N.C.O. of the guard. He also was of opinion that it was a machine-gun, but I remained suspicious in spite of his certainty, and gave orders that I was to be called if the firing seemed to come any nearer. Needless to say, I got no sleep that night, and I was most devoutly thankful when daylight came without untoward incident.

Now for the explanation. The gunfire we had heard came from the volcano of Meru, which has these periodic outbursts of activity, which have been mistaken in the same way by many more than myself. The machine-gun was simply the song of a frog! We afterwards became quite familiar with his note and christened him the "machine-gun frog." Certainly he deserved his name, for a more lifelike imitation of the gun it was impossible to imagine. Anyway, I don't want to hear a better, especially if I happen to be hopelessly mired up in a bush road, with no prospect in case of attack but to scrap it out as long as the ammunition lasts and leave the rest on the knees of the gods.

The next morning dawned upon as hopeless an outlook as need be. The rains had broken this time in good earnest, and as far as the eye could reach the whole country appeared to be literally under wa-ter. Not that it was possible to see much of the country, for the rain was so violent that it was like thick fog. It lay over the landscape as a heavy mist, and the noise of it among the dense foliage was almost deafening—more like the roar of a cataract than anything else. Soon after daylight I went back to look at the cars. These were all sunk deep in the black, holding mud, and it was quite evident that there would be no Aruscha for us until the rains were over. Two of them were so badly mired that they lay almost on their sides, and it was palpable that it would mean very heavy work to get them out, even after the rain should have ceased and the country had begun to dry a little.

The others were not in such bad positions, but were bad enough in all conscience. The great trouble was that they were stretched out over three-quarters of a mile of road, where there was no place to form a camp, and where, had we been attacked, each car would have had to fight its own separate action without being able to move a yard. The position was by no means a pleasant one. though I had no particular fear of being interfered with by the enemy, who was finding his hands pretty full farther away to the south. As a matter of fact, some of his patrols did come within a couple of miles of us, but apparently did not think it was good enough to come near the road.

At any rate, we saw nothing of them during the time we were stuck in the mud, and, truth to tell, I was not at all anxious to make their acquaintance in the circumstances. It being clear that our stay here was to be lengthy, I set out to find a place where the men could be comfortable without running the risk of becoming infected with indigenous disease. Close by was a great coffee plantation, with some sixty thousand trees in full bearing, belonging to a German of some position. He had built himself a substantial stone house a quarter of a mile from the road, and as this promised the only shelter available I had the guns and ammunition taken out of the cars and conveyed to the house, which we put into a state of defence in case of accidents, and left the cars to their fate in the meantime.

It may not have been quite an orthodox line of conduct, but it seemed to me to be the wisest in the circumstances. Already the men were beginning to feel the strain of the unaccustomed climate, combined with the hard work and short commons, and I had several severe cases of dysentery among them, while fever was beginning to appear.

CHAPTER 22

Fighting the Mud

The coffee estate on which we had taken up our quarters was a very extensive one which, in normal times, must have been a very profitable enterprise for its owner. At the time of which I am writing the trees were all in full bearing, and I have never seen a better crop. It would have been almost literally impossible to have got another berry on any tree, so plentiful was the harvest. And they were fine berries, too, with well-developed beans which would have been worth good prices in the market if they could have been dealt with. In the house itself were large bins full of coffee beans, containing, as we estimated, a total of seventy or eighty tons of first-class coffee:—all going to waste because of war's futilities.

Evidently the estate had been very well managed before its owner was called away on active service. In addition to the main crop of coffee, gardens had been laid out near the house in which grew some of the finest roses I had seen for a long time. Almost every one of the familiar garden flowers of the homeland was there. Then there were vegetable and fruit gardens as well, but of the former not much was left—van Deventer's troopers had already visited the place. In the fruit gardens grew every conceivable variety of tropical fruit, from guavas and pomegranates to tree tomatoes, and very welcome they were as a variation of the eternal beef and biscuit that had been our only diet since we left Mbuyuni. It was like an enchanted garden, planted down here in the midst of the rank bush, with a tumbling river wending its course within a hundred yards of the house, and the low hum of the tropical jungle eternally in one's ears, disturbed now and then by the clear, beautifully sweet note of the blacksmith bird, which is for all the world like that of a silver bell. Save for its distance from the haunts of men, it was truly an idyllic spot.

It was no part of our programme, however, to sit down and enjoy the delights of this paradise of the bush for a moment longer than was necessary. Even apart from that, unless we proposed to live on the produce of the fruit gardens, it was becoming essential to get along, since we had almost come to the end of our food resources, and there was no more to be had this side of Aruscha. The rain continued with unabated violence day and night, and it was hopeless even to think about trying to move any of the cars until it should have ceased. The main source of worry as to that was whether the cars would not disappear altogether in the sea of liquid mud which had once been a "road." I had had timber cut and placed under the wheels, so as to lessen the tendency of the heavy armoured vehicles to sink, and also to give us a "take-off" when it became possible to move again; so there was nothing to be done but to exercise what patience we could, pending the return of better weather.

In the meantime I sent one of the officers with a party of men to get through to Aruscha and report on the state of the roads in front and, incidentally, to obtain what he could in the way of supplies. This party returned on the third day, having succeeded in their mission and bringing back sufficient supplies to carry on with for three or four days. They reported that the road over which we had already passed was by way of being a really good highway compared with what we had to traverse farther on—the officer in charge even ventured to doubt whether we should ever get the cars through at all. Apparently, too, they were almost as badly off for supplies in Aruscha as we were, and were dependent on the few pack animal transport columns that could get through from Longido, so that the whole of van Deventer's force had been put on half rations, with the immediate prospect of a reduction to half that.

On the sixth day after our enforced halt the rain ceased for a time, and under the influence of a powerful sun the road began to dry a little. I knew that the conditions were only temporary, and that it would be as well to take advantage of every chance to snatch even a mile while it could be done. By the afternoon the road had become practicable and we began to move. After almost superhuman labour by all the personnel of the battery, we managed to reach a point about half a mile short of the Kidjenge swamp soon after dark and bivouacked there. There had been no rain all day, and the sun set in a clear sky that promised a continuation of the better weather.

But the luck was not to last, for by midnight it was raining as heavily as ever, and by morning it had become very plain that we were to be here for a considerable time longer. It rained with the most extreme violence all the next day, but the following morning broke fine and sunny. We were bivouacked on the slope dropping down to a small stream, which did not appear to offer any particular difficulty for crossing and, although the rains had swollen it to the dimensions of a respectable torrent, I determined to cross while the weather held. Late in the afternoon we essayed the crossing, but the bottom turned out to be as treacherous as the weather itself, and the first car sank over its axles in soft, slimy mud, and was only prevented from going deeper by the fact that it sat down on the under-shield. However, after two hours of hard labour, and with the assistance of a hundred or so natives, we got it clear and up the opposite slope. There was nothing for it but to cut timber and build a bridge before trying the others. As it was now dark this had to be deferred until the morning.

Next day I set one party to work on bridge-building operations, while the rest were employed in cutting wood to corduroy the road on both sides of the stream. All hands worked excellently and before that evening we had the satisfaction of seeing all the cars safely at the top of the opposite slope. We were now getting into difficulties with our petrol supply. I had calculated that the armoured cars ought to do at least three miles to the gallon, so that if we procured fuel on the basis of two miles per gallon we should be prepared for almost any contingency. That I had seen to before we left Moschi, and I had been confident that whatever else happened we should not be stranded for want of petrol. But the appalling conditions of travelling in the mud and slime had falsified all my calculations.

There had been so much "slip" of the driving wheels that the average consumption of the armoured cars had worked out at very little over one mile to the gallon. As an example of this, it may be remarked that a few days later, in crossing the Kidjenge swamp, over which a causeway road of sorts had been made, and which was not more than half a mile wide, the average reading of the mileometers was rather over six miles for the half-mile actually traversed! I sent a party into Aruscha to endeavour to obtain petrol, but there was none there, nor did the supply officer hold out any hope of immediate supplies.

Anyway, the rain had set in again in real earnest, and if we had had all the petrol in East Africa it would not have availed us, for to move a yard was utterly impossible. It was on this day that my old chief, Beves, passed us with the 2nd Brigade *en route* to join van Deventer. I had heard that someone in Aruscha was in possession of a small quantity of petrol, so I enlisted Beves's help to get it, and he promised to give orders that I was to have it. We got it next day—only fourteen gallons, but still enough to get us to Aruscha if the rains would cease and give us the chance for which we were waiting.

For the next four days it rained absolutely without a fine interval, but on the fifth it ceased and the road soon began to get back into something like working order, so, with the assistance of nearly two hundred natives who had been employed in making a corduroy road across the swamp, we started on the passage of the Kidjenge. Among a number of hard days I think this was the worst we experienced. The timber and branches which had gone to the making of the causeway sank under the weight of the cars into the liquid mud and bunched up under the cars, fouling running gear and axles, so that we had to clear it away with bush knives and axes every ten yards or so.

Several times the drag ropes parted and let the natives down the bank in struggling heaps into the black slime of the swamp, until they became semi-mutinous and could only be kept at it by a mixture of cajolery and threats. Officers and men of the battery worked until they were utterly exhausted, striving not only to put their own weight into the job, but to inspire the natives by the force of the white men's example. At last we had our reward, and saw the last of the cars across this really terrible obstacle, and that, fortunately, without a casualty to any of the cars. Why they stood up to the strain I do not know, but they did, and that was all that mattered.

I really thought that our troubles were nearly at an end now, but it is never safe to calculate on anything in East Africa. The rise from the swamp is the last formidable gradient on the road to Aruscha, and as the surface was in passably good condition I thought it would be as well to get all the cars to the top before ceasing work for the night, in case of rain before morning. The first two got up all right, but the third, when nearly at the top, deviated ever so little from the track, with the consequence that the near side wheels broke through the rotten crust and the car turned practically over—the wheels had sunk into a subterranean watercourse. There was nothing to be done that night, and in the morning I borrowed two spans of oxen from the officer in chaise of a passing convoy and hitched them on to the car. The thirty-two oxen tugged and strained for an hour, but could not move the car an inch, so deeply was she embedded in the black mud—and then it began to rain again.

Rain or no rain, the car had to be extricated from its plight. I had no gear of any sort, except the car jacks and axes to deal with emergencies like this; but there it was, and I had to make the best of it. So I told off six of the best men to work with me in getting the car on to an even keel again, while the rest were set to work on timber-cutting—a job at which most of them had become tolerably expert by this time. Gradually, and by very slight degrees, we jacked the car up by sinking blocks of timber in the watercourse, working most of the time lying down in a foot of running water, and after twelve hours of ceaseless labour we got the car upright and standing on planks placed across the chasm in the road.

By this time it was raining so heavily that it had become manifest that there was to be no movement of cars for some time. Next morning the road had become the bed of a howling torrent, and where two days before had been a level surface there now ran a stream three feet deep by actual measurement. This had been caused by a rather considerable stream a mile farther on having burst its banks and taken the line of least resistance, which was down the centre of the road.

So we set to work on yet another unaccustomed job—that of repairing the damaged banks and the diversion of the main stream to its original course. We succeeded pretty well in this, but not before it had practically obliterated a full mile of the road and made a hollow watercourse of it, which entailed a full two days' woodcutting and filling operations in order to make it practicable when the weather should at last make it possible to move again. It was another eight days before this happened, and in the meantime I was getting seriously concerned about the health of the men. They were all young, and most of them town-dwellers fresh from England, few of them ever having slept in the open before, and the hard work and short commons—we had now been on alleged quarter rations for more than a fortnight—were beginning to tell their tale. Forty *per cent*. of them had either fever or dysentery, and there was not a day but I had to send one or two into Aruscha to hospital.

My own private stock of medicines—I had no official stock of these, they were "not on my establishment"—had long since been exhausted and no more were available, so that I began to think that even if we were fated to reach Aruscha at all in this life it would be to leave the bones of the battery there. We were only a little more than a mile from there now—the longest mile in all my experience—and if only we could get one fine day to dry the roads and renew the hearts of us all! We were all feeling the strain, and I confess that I was myself approaching that state of "fed-up-ness" in which one does not care particularly what happens.

And still it rained pitilessly and continuously, as though it never meant to stop. Never will any of us forget the abject misery of those weeks of abortive effort, when we worked like convicts, fed like animals, and sheltered where we could like the beasts of the bush. But all things have an end, and we were now getting in sight of the goal. Reports came down from the North that the rains had ceased in the Longido district, which meant that they would not be with us much longer, and that with the drying up of the country we should once more be able to move with freedom.

As I have said, we were stuck for eight days within a mile of Aruscha, but on the ninth it became practicable to move again, and we reached a point within five hundred yards of the outskirts of the town, but it was to be yet another week before we could get all the cars into the place itself, so utterly impracticable had the roads become for any species of wheeled traffic.

On the tenth day, by dint of much woodcutting and road-building, we actually managed to get the first armoured car into Aruscha. That was late in the evening, and during the night the rain came again and undid most of the good work we had done on the road, and we had to start all over again. Next day we got another car in, but only just in time, for as it got to the top of the hill in Aruscha itself a violent storm of wind and rain, almost the worst we had experienced, broke and the road became a raging torrent again, and the rain continued practically during the whole of the night.

It had been my intention to get the rest of the cars in next day, whatever the trouble or difficulty, and I had given orders that work was ta begin as soon as the sun had gathered enough strength to make an impression on the surface of the road. There was a bad place, under an avenue of plantains, through which we had only got the first cars with difficulty, but as I had arranged for the help of a gang of natives I did not anticipate very much trouble in negotiating it with the remainder. In the worst part it was rather more than a foot deep, with soft-mud bottom, which we had filled up with sections of plantain trunks to prevent the wheels from sinking too deeply.

While we were getting things ready some pack-bullocks came down the road. One of these animals stepped into the hole, which was full of water, and almost disappeared. What had happened was that the water carried by the spongy, saturated soil had run down underground and simply scooped out our hole until it was between four and five feet deep. Such are East African roads in the rainy season!

It was obvious that this part of the road was of no use to us, and there was nothing for it but to cut another through the bush and corduroy it. That meant another three days' toil, and even then our troubles were by no means at an end. The black cotton soil was so rotten and spongy that even when the track was laid with logs it could not be trusted. When at last it seemed practicable we essayed to move the first car. All went well for about a couple of hundred yards, when one side of the track subsided under the weight of the car, which slid bodily sideways and sank slowly into the ground until brought up by the frame. Once again began the labour of digging for a foundation to afford leverage for the jacks and the interminable cutting of wood for securing the inch or two gained by each lift. It took a day's hard work to get the car upright, but even then it was impossible to move it until the damage to the track had been made good.

Next day more heavy rain fell, rendering it out of the question to move. The one saving aspect of the situation was that the men were able to sleep under cover in the town, and that the sick were able to get proper attention. Once more the weather cleared towards night, and the following day opened with bright sunshine and steamy tropical heat, and everything being ready we set out to move the remaining cars in. Our luck was still out, though, for at about nine o'clock a terrific downpour started, which lasted for about two hours and made moving impossible for that day. However, two days later we did at last manage to get the rest of the battery vehicles to Aruscha, looking very much the worse for wear and needing some little attention to details, but still not a single car had broken down except the abandoned lorry, and none of them was otherwise than fit to go through the same again.

We had been just five weeks in covering the distance from Mbuyuni, a distance that we could easily have covered in a day over roads worthy of the name. Indeed, except for the Kidjenge swamp, which was a perfect nightmare, we could have done the journey in three days with the greatest ease in the dry season. As it was, I really do not know how we ever got through it at all. I thought I had learnt all there was to know about moving armoured cars in bad country during the campaign in South-West Africa, but heavy sand is a mere trifle compared with the black cotton mud of that road to Aruscha. There are some things that can be circumvented by ingenuity, and others that can be defeated by simple determination and force, but the East African mud will not be denied. As a matter of fact, I think we were entitled to congratulate ourselves on having got through at all, since the road we were on was closed even to pack animal transport by the time we had been a fortnight on it, as it was judged to be impracticable for transport of any kind.

After our arrival at Aruscha the cars were overhauled in readiness for the move on the Central Railway under van Deventer, who was now at Kondoa Irangi, where the battery joined him on the 23rd of May, though the advance to the railway was not to begin until more than a month later. Before that could be consummated a considerable redistribution of troops took place, in view of the altered dispositions of the enemy, and it was then that my association in the field with armoured cars came to an end.

★★★★★★

I have campaigned in various places with every arm of the service, but I have never done more interesting work than with these cars. One thing I have acquired as a consequence, and that is an abiding faith in the armoured car as an adjunct of modern war. Faster than cavalry in good open country; impervious to anything but a direct hit from guns; self-contained whether as a unit or a battery; with a commanding fire effect, and, what is perhaps its most valuable characteristic, a tremendous moral effect on the enemy and on our own men who are working with it, it is a most valuable offensive weapon in a country in which it has any freedom of movement. To ensure that freedom it is not necessary to have roads, for the people who know their business can almost literally take armoured cars anywhere—except through deep mud.

In this war, and in the wars of the future, the armoured car, as distinct altogether from the vehicle of the "Tank" type, will play a most important part, especially when its real functions are better understood and appreciated.

CHAPTER 23

The "Eviction" Phase

It has already been recorded that at the time we reached Aruscha van Deventer was at Kondoa Irangi, threatening the enemy's main line of railway at Kilimatinde and already dominating the high, fertile plateau which connects Aruscha with the Central Railway. Moreover, he had occupied the dominant strategic points for any further advance, whether this should be in the direction of the railway, westwards to the new capital, Tabora, or eastwards to Handeni and the Usambara.

This potent threat brought the German commander-in-chief, Colonel von Lettow, on the scene, with a strong force which he had hurriedly transferred from the Usambara. By the time his arrangements were complete he was able to dispose of about four thousand men for the purpose of dealing with the 2nd Division, which was so weakened by sickness that van Deventer could hardly put 3,000 rifles in the line.

The Germans attacked the position in front of Kondoa Irangi on May 7th, and fighting continued intermittently until the 9th, when the enemy made his great effort. Between seven o'clock on the 9th and three a.m. on the 10th four attacks were made and pressed gallantly home, the Germans and their *askaris* in some cases charging right up to our positions. The brunt of the fighting fell on the 11th and 12th South African Infantry, who stood their ground right well, each separate attack being repulsed with loss to the enemy. After the failure of the fourth attack the enemy withdrew, leaving a number of his dead and wounded on the ground in front of the South Africans.

In the language of Smuts's dispatch dealing with this phase of the operations, with this defeat the enemy's last hope of successful resistance to any large portion of our forces was extinguished. He continued in position in front of Kondoa Irangi during the remainder of

May and the greater part of June, keeping for the most part to the thick bush, and engaging in desultory fighting and long-range bombardment. General van Deventer was unable to assume the offensive on account of the loss of most of his horses through "fly" and horse-sickness, the heavy sick-rate among the men, and the difficulties of supply along a line of communication represented by two hundred miles of quagmire.

The ceasing of the rains in the middle of May made possible the initiation of a movement for the clearing of the enemy from the Pare and Usambara Hills. The "general idea" was to move south-east along the line of these hills and then, opposite Handeni, to swing south and strike for the Central Railway on a line parallel to van Deventer's advance farther to the west. The movement began on May 12th with the advance of the 3rd King's African Rifles from Mbuyuni to the Ngulu Gap, followed on the 22nd by Hannyngton's brigade from the Ruwu, following the line of the Usambara railway, and the brigades of Sheppard and Beves down the Pangani River.

The story of the advance of these columns is a monotonous one of arduous marching under the worst of conditions. Thick bush, little food and much sickness among the troops sum up the salient features of this phase of the campaign. There was some amount of fighting, it is true, but here again the genius of the commander-in-chief was seen at its best. To select one example of his manner of conduct in the operations, his own description of the capture of the enemy's position at Mikotscheni, on the Pangani, may be cited. He says in his dispatch:

> On May 29th the advanced troops came up against this position and drew fire from a naval 4.1-inch gun and two field-guns. On May 30th the 2nd Rhodesian Regiment attacked the position in front, while the rest of General Sheppard's brigade made an arduous but successful turning movement by our left. The enemy retired during the night, leaving part of a new bridge in process of construction behind him.

It was always thus—just as everything seemed ripe for decision the enemy slipped out through the only bolt-hole open to him.

By the end of the third week in June the initial object of the operations had been attained and the enemy driven out of the Pare and Usambara hills, with the exception of a small area in the east. The troops had suffered severely from malaria—some of the units being reduced to 80 per cent. of their original strength. Since the end of May they

158

had marched over two hundred miles in the most difficult country, often having to cut their way through almost impenetrable bush, and had constantly engaged the enemy in his prepared rearguard positions. Taking all things into consideration, Smuts decided that the movement must slow down and that, in view of the difficulties of transport and supply, the Mombo-Nderema trolley line must be repaired before moving farther. Moreover, it was essential to his ultimate plans that the 2nd Division under van Deventer should be more advanced before the combined movement against the Central Railway should begin. A large standing camp was, therefore, formed on the Msiha River, eight miles beyond Lukigura, in which to rest and refit the troops before the next phase of the operations.

While the main force was resting Tanga was occupied by a combined land and sea operation, after very slight opposition from an enemy force of about two companies. Opportunity was also taken to clear out the small hostile detachments that were hanging about in the area between the left flank of our main forces and the sea. This was successfully accomplished, the navy co-operating most effectively and occupying the ports of Pangani, Sadani Bay and Bagamoyo. At the last named place one of the "four-point-ones" landed from the cruiser *Königsberg* was captured, the Germans, for a wonder, leaving it in perfect working order with a good supply of ammunition.

By the end of July the situation had de veloped in such a manner that it was possible to resume the advance of the main force. The Central Railway had been occupied by van Deventer from Kondoa Irangi to Dodoma; all the coast towns as far south as Sadani had been taken; in the lake area a combined British and Belgian force was preparing to move on Tabora; and in the south General Northey's force from Nyasaland was beginning to make its presence felt.

The enemy's main forces were in the Ngulu and Kanga mountains, where they were skilfully disposed in a series of well-prepared positions which would have entailed bitter fighting to take by direct assault. When the time was ripe Smuts simply carried out his favourite manoeuvre of wide turning movements, which had the effect of causing the enemy to retire southwards with some precipitancy lest worse should befall. There was some stiff fighting at Matamondo and on the Wami River, in which the enemy was severely handled. Van Deventer, too, came in for his share of the fighting, and fought two smart actions at Mpapua and Kidete, inflicting serious losses on the retiring Germans.

It had been confidently expected that the foe would make a really determined stand at Morogoro, the surrounding country being admirably adapted for defensive operations. But once more, by prompt resort to wide turning movements, the Germans were hustled out of Morogoro, which was occupied on August 26th, the enemy leaving many evidences of a precipitate and demoralised flight.

In spite of the exhaustion of men and animals consequent upon three weeks of the most trying marching and almost continuous fighting. Smuts decided to give the flying enemy no rest, and arrangements were at once carried out for continuing the pursuit to the south. This pursuit was pressed in spite of the most appalling difficulties of country and roads, and in face of the most determined opposition. There were very few days on which our troops were not more or less seriously engaged with the German rearguards, but by the middle of September the decisive phases of the campaign may be said to have been over, and the enemy's main forces were in full retreat for the delta of the Rufiji River.

In the meantime the navy had been carrying out operations against the coast, in combination with a land force of about 1,800 rifles, and Dar-es-Salaam, the principal port and original capital of the German colony, had been occupied on September 4th. Before leaving the place the Germans had destroyed the railway station and harbour works, and had sunk four steamers, only one of which it was found profitable to salve. Subsequently the whole of the coast towns were occupied, and the entire littoral was in British occupation by the end of September.

Another severe blow to the enemy's prestige was dealt by the combined British-Belgian column which, it has been said, was advancing from Lake Tanganyika, This was the capture of Tabora, which was occupied on September 19th with comparatively slight opposition, the enemy retiring eastwards with the obvious intention of joining hands with the main forces withdrawing to the delta of the Rufiji.

By the latter part of September, therefore, the essential part of Smuts's task had been satisfactorily accomplished. There still remained a great deal of clearing up to be done, but so far as the successful conquest of the last remaining German colony was concerned, this was to be regarded as already *un fait accompli*. The enemy had been driven south over the Central Railway, the whole of which was in our hands. In the east he was entirely cut off from the coast; the single valuable area left to him being the relatively small Mahenge plateau, which was threatened by Northey's advance from the south-west; the Portuguese were pressing him north of the Rovuma River; van Deventer was harrying the portion of the German force which was retreating from Tabora, and was on the point of joining hands with Northey; and the main body was hard put to it to evade the pressure of the 1st and 3rd Divisions which were under the personal direction of the commander-in-chief.

Subsequent operations, which led to the virtual internment of the enemy forces in the Rufiji delta, one of the most unhealthy districts of East Africa, are of only subsidiary interest, and there is no occasion to follow them, particularly as the fate of the colony had been definitely settled by the operations that have been briefly sketched already.

German East Africa had been wrested from a resourceful enemy by a series of operations as brilliantly conceived and carried out as any in the annals of tropical war, consummated by the genius of a great soldier and the magnificent qualities of the troops. In commenting upon the work of his men, Smuts himself says:

> Their work has been done under tropical conditions which not only produce bodily weariness and unfitness, but which create mental languor and depression and, finally, appal the stoutest hearts. To march day by day, and week by week, through the African jungle or high grass, in which vision is limited to a few yards, in which danger always lurks near but seldom becomes visible, even when experienced, supplies a test to human nature often in the long run beyond the limits of human endurance.

I have heard it said, not once but many times, that these "side-shows" of the Great War have been in the nature of picnics. It may be that, compared with the magnitude of the operations on the main European fronts, they have been relatively small affairs, but the reader can now form his own judgment as to whether the African campaigns deserve to be so contemptuously described.